The Lucent Library of Historical Eras

The Ancient Greeks
at Home and at Work

Other titles in the Lucent Library of Historical Eras include:

Ancient Greece:
A History of the Ancient Greeks
Leisure Life of the Ancient Greeks
Philosophy and Science in Ancient Greece: The Pursuit of Knowledge

Elizabethan England:
Elizabeth I and Her Court
Great Elizabethan Playwrights
A History of the Elizabethan Theater
Life in Elizabethan London
Primary Sources

Ancient Rome:
Arts, Leisure, and Entertainment: Life of the Ancient Romans
From Founding to Fall: A History of Rome
Influential Figures of Ancient Rome
The Roman Army: An Instrument of Power
Words of the Ancient Romans: Primary Sources

The Lucent Library of Historical Eras

The Ancient Greeks at Home and at Work

Don Nardo

LUCENT
BOOKS®

THOMSON
★
™
GALE

San Diego • Detroit • New York • San Francisco • Cleveland • New Haven, Conn. • Waterville, Maine • London • Munich

THOMSON

GALE

LIBRARY OF CONGRESS CATALOGING-IN-PUBLICATION DATA

Nardo, Don, 1947–
   The ancient Greeks at home and at work / by Don Nardo.
      p. cm. — (The Lucent library of historical eras. Ancient Greece)
   Includes bibliographical references.
   ISBN 1-59018-526-9
   1. Greece—Social life and customs—Juvenile literature. I. Title. II. Series.
   DF91.N37 2004
   938—dc22
                                                    2004006303

Printed in the United States of America

Contents

Foreword

Looking back from the vantage point of the present, history can be viewed as a myriad of intertwining roads paved by human events. Some paths stand out—broad highways whose mileposts, even from a distance of centuries, are clear. The events that propelled the rise to power of Germany's Third Reich, its role in World War II, and its eventual demise, for example, are well defined and documented.

Other roads are less distinct, their route sometimes hidden from view. Modern legislatures may have developed from old tribal councils, for example, but the links between them are indistinct in places, open to discussion and interpretation.

The architecture of civilization—law, religion, art, science, and government—as well as the more everyday aspects of our culture—what we eat, what we wear—all developed along the historical roads and byways. In that progression can be traced every facet of modern life.

A broad look back along these roads reveals that many paths—though of vastly different character—seem to converge at a few critical junctions. These intersections are those great historical eras that echo over the long, steady course of human history, extending beyond the past and into the present.

These epic periods of time are the focus of Lucent's Library of Historical Eras. They shine through the mists of history like beacons, illuminated by a burst of creativity that propels events forward—so bright that we, from thousands of years away, can clearly see the chain of events leading to the present.

Each Lucent Library of Historical Eras consists of a set of books that highlight various aspects of these major eras. For example, the Elizabethan England library features volumes on Queen Elizabeth I and her court, Elizabethan theater, the great playwrights, and everyday life in Elizabethan London.

The mini-library approach allows for the division of each era into its most significant and most interesting parts and the exploration of those parts in depth. Also, social and cultural trends as well as illustrative documents and eyewitness accounts can be prominently featured in individual volumes.

Lucent's Library of Historical Eras presents a wealth of information to young readers. The lively narrative, fully documented primary and secondary source quotations, maps, photographs, sidebars, and annotated bibliographies serve as launching points for class discussion and further research.

In studying the great historical eras, students also develop a better understanding of our own times. What we learn from the past and how we apply it in the present may shape the future and may determine whether our era will be a guiding light to those traveling future roads.

Introduction:
The Mute Stones Speak: Evidence for Greek Life

When describing any aspect of the ancient world, historians are always at the mercy of the surviving evidence. The sad fact is that more than 90 percent of all the writings produced by ancient peoples have been lost. And most of their physical artifacts either have been obliterated over the centuries or else lie buried in unknown places or beneath the streets and buildings of modern cities, where they cannot be found or excavated easily. Moreover, the ravages of time, natural erosion, and human destruction and construction have not erased the past in even-handed, consistent ways. Gaps of all sizes and kinds exist in the historical record. Sometimes a fair amount of evidence survives from one site or town, but the remains of nearby sites are scarce or nonexistent. Or scholars have abundant evidence for a people, nation, or city in a certain narrow time period but have extremely little evidence for the periods preceding and following that era.

Such is the case, in large degree, for many ancient Greek sites. Evidence is especially uneven and unclear for some aspects of Greece's social history, that is, its houses and home life; social classes, customs, and institutions, including religion and slavery; and the occupations and habits of its people. Today the phrase "ancient Greece" tends to conjure up visions of Athens, with the magnificent ruins of the Parthenon and other temples atop its central hill, the Acropolis. This is no accident. Athens was for many centuries the most populous, famous, and influential of the Greek city-states (which viewed themselves as separate tiny nations). And most of the substantial firsthand information that has survived about Greek civilization comes from Athenian writers and other Athenian sources and describes Athenian history, customs, and ideas.

This does not mean that other Greek states did not have rich cultures of their own. They did. But few remains of those cultures have survived. For example, the venerable and splendid city of Thebes (situated north of Athens) was sacked and wrecked numerous times in antiquity, leaving only a few pitiful walls and building foundations for future generations to study and learn from. The same can be said of Corinth (west of Athens), which once rivaled Athens in prosperity. The Romans reduced Corinth to rubble in the second century B.C.; the city was later rebuilt, but barbarian invaders and earthquakes finished it off in the early Christian era. The vast majority of records and native writings of these cities also perished.

Athens: "An Education to Greece"

In contrast, along with many writings by Athenian writers, large portions of Athens itself survived the centuries more or less intact (although many of its public buildings and most of its houses disintegrated over time or were covered by later structures). Yet though these survivals are fortunate, they are also problematic. Historians are often forced to draw conclusions about life in other Greek cities based primarily on evidence found in Athens, when in truth it is sometimes difficult to know whether certain Athenian institutions, customs, and beliefs were unique to that city or could be applied just as well to most other Greek states. As a result, caution must be used when examining life in ancient Greece. In the words of Thomas R. Martin of the College of the Holy Cross:

> The state of the surviving evidence, which consistently comes more from Athens than from other city-states, and the focus of modern popular interest in ancient Greece, which has traditionally remained on the magnificent cultur-

al remains of Athens, have combined to push Greek history . . . mightily in the direction of Athenian history. This limitation must be kept in mind so that one can avoid the trap of substituting "Greece" for "Athens" when talking about [the ancient world].[1]

Still, at least in general terms, Athenian culture was likely fairly typical of greater

The Athenian Acropolis as seen from the air. The largest structure on the summit is the Parthenon.

Greek culture, partly because Athens was so famous and influential. A number of important institutions, including democracy, theater, and drama, originated in Athens and subsequently were adopted by other Greek states. Indeed, in many ways Athens became a trendsetter and a model that other states were eager to follow. Though obviously biased, a noted statement made by the fifth-century B.C. Athenian leader Pericles had a strong element of truth in it. "I declare that our city is an education to Greece," he said. "The present age wonders at us . . . [and] our adventurous spirit has forced an entry into every sea and into every land."[2] Also, putting the matter of Athens's influence aside, it appears that dress styles, farming and military methods, trade, athletics, basic occupations, and core religious beliefs and practices were largely the same across the Greek world.

There are exceptions to every rule, of course. In the case of overall Greek cultural standards and practices, the major exception was the city-state of Sparta, located in the Peloponnesus (the large peninsula making up the southernmost third of the Greek mainland). A fair amount of information has survived about Spartan society and customs. And most of it does not come from surviving Spartan writings (of which there were few to begin with) but rather from the works

A modern drawing depicts ancient Sparta, in the southern part of the Peloponnesus. Spartan customs differed significantly from those of other Greek states.

of other Greeks. Among the more important of these were the Athenian historian Thucydides (fifth century B.C.); the Athenian philosopher and scholar Aristotle (fourth century B.C.); the historian Herodotus (fifth century B.C., from Halicarnassus, on the western coast of Asia Minor, what is now Turkey); and the biographer and moralist Plutarch (first century A.D., from Boeotia, the region lying north of the Athenian territory of Attica). Sparta was a major and compelling subject for these and other Greek, as well as Roman, writers. This is because its entire society was constructed around a unique, very regimented system of military training, which turned out the best and most feared soldiers in Greece. Owing to Sparta's importance to the rest of Greece for a number of crucial centuries, its unusual social institutions and customs must be considered alongside those of Athens and other Greek states that had more traditional cultures.

The phrase "crucial centuries" is a reminder that the particular time period in which a state existed is as important to the discussion of ancient Greek life as the question of whether that state was culturally typical or atypical. Just as most of the surviving cultural evidence comes from Athens, a large proportion of the Athenian evidence comes from the Classical Age. This was the period that modern scholars reckon from about 500 B.C., shortly after Athens established its democracy—the world's first—to 323 B.C., the year the Macedonian Greek conqueror Alexander the Great died.

The point is that both before and after this era, Greek society did not remain static. Rather, it steadily evolved and changed, just as modern society does (although the rate of change was much slower in ancient times than it is now, thanks to modern technological advances). For example, marriage customs, educational opportunities, and artistic styles were extremely different in 1000 B.C., when Greece languished in an impoverished, culturally backward state, than in Classical times, when Athens enjoyed its so-called golden age. And the treatment of and opportunities for Greek women were considerably better in most parts of Greece in the centuries following the Classical Age (an era that scholars call the Hellenistic Age, when Greek civilization spread across much of the Near East). Unfortunately, the other ancient periods are not as well documented as the Classical Age in most areas, so modern discussions of ancient Greek life, including this one, focus mostly on that crucial period. Nevertheless, the institutions, social roles, customs, and beliefs of other ancient Greek eras must be described when necessary or relevant.

Two Kinds of Evidence

Whatever the era in question, evidence for home and work life in Athens, Sparta, and other ancient Greek states takes two main forms. First are the written sources, to the extent that they exist in certain places and times. In addition to Herodotus, Thucydides, Aristotle, and Plutarch, other Greek writers whose works shed light on social history include the Athenian Xenophon (ZEN-uh-phon, fourth century B.C.), who discussed farming and the duties of women and slaves,

Euripides and the other great fifth-century B.C. Athenian playwrights, whose works captured or reflected contemporary social mores, customs, and religious beliefs, and the treatises of Aristotle's mentor and fellow scholar Plato, whose dialogues discuss social classes, the home, religion, and morality. Also valuable are several surviving speeches from the Athenian law courts. These were written by professional writers and orators for average citizens pleading their cases. They reveal not only much legal information but also numerous facts about the home, family relationships, occupations, and other major aspects of everyday life.

Supporting the written sources, which by no means cover all aspects of Greek life, is the archaeological evidence. One important example consists of inscriptions—words carved onto stone, wood, and other hard surfaces. Of these, tomb epitaphs are particularly revealing because they are often the principal source of knowledge about the lives and feelings of those who had no political power or voice—women, children, and slaves. An epitaph found at Athens's port town, Piraeus, which dates from about 360 B.C., at the height of the Classical Age, captures the grief of a mother for her lost son and confirms that familial relationships could be as close as the closest known today:

Xenoclea, daughter of Nicarchus, lies here dead. She mourned the sad end of her son, Phoenix, who died out at sea when he was eight years old. There is no one so ignorant of grief, Xenoclea, that doesn't pity your fate. . . . [You] died of grief for your son, who has a pitiless tomb where he lies in the dark sea.[3]

Other kinds of archaeological evidence include tools; plates, cups, and cooking utensils; combs, mirrors, and other grooming items; coins; statues and paintings; skeletons and other human remains; and remnants of buildings. Regarding the latter, one of the most important excavations in modern times took place at the site of ancient Olynthus, in northern Greece, during the 1920s and 1930s. There an American expedition led by D.M. Robinson uncovered the remains of more than a hundred houses dating from the Classical Age. The warlike Macedonian king Philip II (Alexander's father), ordered the destruction of the city in 348 B.C., but fortunately, few later structures were erected on the spot, so the houses' foundations remained intact under a layer of earth. Also discovered in the ruins were vases, lamps, kitchenware, mosaics, bathtubs, grain mills, coins, and hundreds of other items.

In this way, the mute stones can speak and help scholars in their attempt to piece together a faithful picture of Greek home and community life. That picture remains imperfect. But excavations continue at sites all over Greece. Archaeologists and historians are particularly hopeful about the huge potential for new knowledge from excavations at Helike, a city that lies buried on the northern coast of the Peloponnesus. An earthquake and tsunami suddenly submerged Helike in 373 B.C. Archaeologists rediscovered it in 2001, and many have come to call it the "Greek Pompeii," in reference to the famous Roman town that was buried and preserved largely intact by a volcanic eruption in A.D. 79. Years of excavations at Pompeii have provided a treasure trove of valuable information about the homes and shops of ordinary Romans. If Helike fulfills its similar potential, in the years to come it will open new and illuminating windows on how the Greeks, the founders of Western civilization, lived and worked.

Chapter 1

Houses: Their Structure, Layout, and Contents

The Athenian historian Xenophon, who flourished in the early fourth century B.C., at the height of the Classical Age, estimated that Athens had some ten thousand houses in his day. All of these family dwellings are now gone. Substantial portions of the city's famous temples and other public buildings have survived the ravages of time, but only the foundations of a few of the homes of those who erected these great monuments remain. What were houses like during Greece's greatest age? Can we assume that people enjoyed the same degree of splendor in their private lives that they lavished on the monuments they erected to their gods?

The answer to the last question is a resounding no. In fact, the vast majority of Athenian houses, including those of well-to-do families, were simple in design and smaller and more modestly furnished than the average modern middle-class home. In one of his speeches, the fourth-century B.C. Athenian orator Demosthenes calls attention to the relative simplicity of the residences of Pericles and other leading generals and politicians of the previous century:

The [public] buildings which they left behind them to adorn our city—temples, harbors, and their accessories—were so great and so fair that we who come after must despair of ever surpassing them. . . . But the private houses of those who rose to power . . . are not a whit more splendid than those of their neighbors.[4]

Demosthenes goes on to say that in his own day a number of leading citizens had built more spacious and attractive homes. Yet these larger residences remained unusual; indeed, part of the reason the orator called attention to them was that they were so uncommon. Twentieth-century excavations of blocks of residences at Olynthus, in northern Greece, show clearly that most Greek houses of that period were small and modest. In his classic book on ancient Greek town planning, scholar R.E. Wycherley sums it up this way:

Classical Greek houses were mostly unpretentious, at least from the outside. They were hardly expected to

This reconstruction shows ancient townhouses lining a main street in a Greek city. Such homes were typically modest in size and decoration.

make much contribution to the architectural beauty of the city. . . . The Greeks of the fifth century [B.C.] put their best, architecturally, into temples and public buildings, and were content with modest private dwellings. . . . The agora [marketplace], the shrines, the theater, the gymnasia, and so forth occupied sites determined by traditional sanctity or convenience. The houses filled in the rest. There was little possibility of [a house having] a spacious layout or a generous allocation of ground. The ordinary Greek urban house had little room . . . [because the] narrow streets and houses huddled together . . . conditions intolerable by modern standards.[5]

Thus, if no traces of the Parthenon and other large-scale Athenian public structures had survived, modern researchers might have concluded that Athens was a primitive, backward town. In truth, it was anything but backward for its day. Yet most of its residents were perfectly willing to live in modest dwellings, at least modest in size and degree of outer ornamentation. More important to understanding ancient Greek home life is what the interior layout and contents of these houses were like. How many rooms did they have? Did they have cooking and bathroom facilities? How were they heated, and where did the residents get their water? Excavations at Olynthus, in various parts of the Athenian territory of Attica, at Priene (a Greek city on the coast of Asia

Socrates on Why Houses Should Face South

In this excerpt from Xenophon's Memorabilia *(in* Xenophon: Conversations of Socrates*), in which he fondly recalls his friend the philosopher Socrates, the latter explains why facing a house toward the south can make the family that dwells in it more comfortable.*

If a man is to have the sort of house he needs, ought he to contrive to make it as pleasant and convenient as possible to live in? . . . Isn't it pleasant to have a house which is cool in summer and warm in winter? . . . Well, in houses that have a south [facing] aspect, in winter the sun shines into the [courtyards], while in summer it passes over our heads and over the roof and casts a shade. So, if this is the desired effect, one should build the south side higher so as not to shut off the winter sun, and the north side lower so as to avoid exposure to cold winds. In short, the most pleasant and fine residence is likely to be that which offers at all seasons the most agreeable retreat for the owner.

Some country homes in ancient Greece were villas like this one. Villas sometimes doubled as organizational centers of large farms.

Minor), and elsewhere have provided at least partial answers to these and other questions about what home life was like in Greece in Classical times.

Country Houses

One important factor that affected the lifestyle of a Greek family was the location of its home. As is still true in modern societies, some Greeks lived in cities and others in the countryside. However, there were no modern-style suburbs—that is, large clusters of homes with their own shopping areas and public squares lying just outside the cities. Instead, a typical city had a stout defensive wall that sharply marked its outer

boundary. Beyond the wall stretched large expanses of countryside punctuated here and there by small villages and farmhouses. So, one lived either in crowded, noisy urban surroundings or in quiet rural settings, as there was usually nothing to speak of in between.

Another difference between the ancient Greek world and the modern one was the way the population was distributed between city and country. Today, there are few farmers and most people live in cities or suburbs. In Greece (and other ancient lands), by contrast, agriculture was the mainstay of the economy, and farming was by far the most common profession. Therefore, more

A father greets his wife and daughter on his way to the courtyard in this large house. Most Greek homes were much smaller.

people lived in the countryside than in the cities. For instance, recent studies suggest that 60 percent of Boeotians lived in the rural villages and farms surrounding the major Greek city of Thebes.

The houses in which these rural Greeks dwelled varied according to need and circumstance. Some farmers maintained their families in small villages, each consisting of a few modest huts clustered together for mutual security. These farmers arose early each morning and walked to their fields. Other farmers lived in huts erected right beside their fields. Whether inside or outside of a village, a typical rural house was made of wood, fieldstones, sun-dried clay bricks, or maybe a combination of these materials. Such a structure had one, two, or three rooms, with floors of hard-packed dirt, sometimes covered by flagstones or straw mats. A crude stone-lined hearth in the main room provided heat and cooking facilities.

Larger, more comfortable country homes, generally referred to as villas, were fewer in number because most people could not afford to build and maintain them. A villa usually consisted of a group of perhaps five to ten rooms lining the perimeter of a central courtyard that was open to the sky and elements. The villas excavated to date were primarily residences rather than working farmhouses. A person who could afford a villa could also afford to construct separate structures for storing grain, pressing olives, housing livestock, and so forth, all probably well away from the main house.

Evidence suggests that most villas, and probably some ordinary farmhouses as well, had stone defensive towers, perhaps ten to fifteen feet high. A family living well outside the city's protective walls needed a safe refuge to escape to in case of sudden danger. A villa with such a tower, dated to between 350 and 300 B.C., in late Classical times, was uncovered during the early 1970s near modern Vari, south of Athens. And the remains of a number of other such towers have since been found in other parts of Attica.

Townhouses: Materials and Layout

Houses in cities resembled rural houses in some ways. A typical Greek townhouse featured a stone foundation and walls made of sun-dried clay bricks. Wooden timbers were sometimes used to reinforce the bricks. But the walls were still not very strong or durable. The earthen bricks began to crumble after a few years, forcing homeowners to undertake frequent repairs. Also, it was extremely easy for thieves to tunnel through such walls. According to Plutarch, Demosthenes once remarked, "You Athenians should not be surprised at the number of thefts that are committed, when we have thieves of brass [great nerve], while the walls of our houses are only made of clay."[6] Indeed, in Athens thieves tunneled through walls so often that burglars

there became known as *toichorhychoi,* or "wall piercers."

Because space in cities like Athens was at a premium, the houses were crammed together along narrow, winding streets. The fronts of these dwellings were usually plain and whitewashed, each with a single door and no more than one or two small windows. The windows were located well above street level so that no one could easily see or crawl inside. As for the doors, they opened outward. To make sure they did not strike passersby, they were narrow, and for added measure it was customary for a person leaving the house to give a loud knock to warn people in the street. The only decoration in the front of a townhouse was a *herm,* a bust of the god Hermes sitting on a pedestal about three or four feet high, near the door. Hermes was the patron deity of travelers, and it was believed that his likeness kept evil from entering the house. Whenever possible, the fronts of houses faced south. Xenophon explains why in his *Memorabilia:* "In houses that have a south [facing] aspect, in winter the sun shines into the courtyards, while in summer it passes over our heads and over the roof and casts a [cooling] shade."[7]

Judging from the evidence from Olynthus, Priene, and elsewhere, the layout, or ground plans, of Greek townhouses were extremely varied. Many had rooms grouped around a small central courtyard, but not necessarily in an even or symmetrical fashion. In others, most rooms opened into a long central hallway called a *pastas.* The very poorest homes had perhaps two rooms, but the average house had four to seven small rooms and a few larger residences had more; one Olynthian home, dubbed the House of Zoilus by excavators, had more than seventeen rooms.

The ground plan of a wealthy home, which included two inner courtyards (A and B) lined with pillars (represented by black circles).

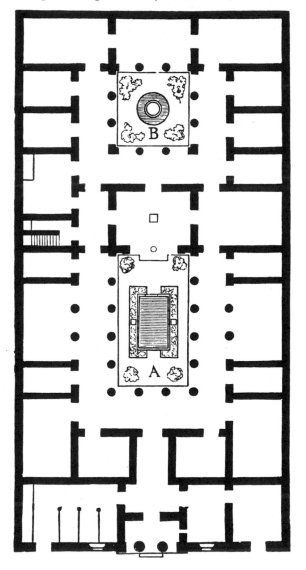

Wycherley summarizes the varying layouts of the Greek houses uncovered in recent times:

> [Many were] built round a small courtyard and looked inwards toward this rather than outwards toward the streets and their neighbors. Each was self-contained and turned in on itself. . . . In certain types [which were common at Priene] there was one dominant room which gave the impression of being the nucleus of the whole, and the other rooms and the courtyard itself appeared as appendages. In other types this emphasis was absent. . . . [At Olynthus] the *pastas* [extended] across the whole or nearly the whole of the house, with a series of other rooms opening on to it from the north. In the middle of the south side was a small court. . . . The *pastas* opened onto the court through a row of three or four pillars. . . . The houses [at Olynthus] had no dominant room. [8]

Another variation in layout was that some houses had only a ground floor, but others had two (and occasionally three) stories. Part of the evidence for this comes from a courtroom speech penned by the Athenian orator Lysias between 400 and 380 B.C. He had the defendant in the case, Euphiletus, say that his house had two floors, the lower floor devoted to the men of the family, and the upper floor to the women.

Upstairs, Downstairs in a Greek House

The Athenian orator Lysias wrote a now-famous speech for the defense of a man named Euphiletus, who was brought to trial for killing a man whom he caught in bed with his wife. This portion of the speech (from Kathleen Freeman's The Murder of Herodes) *provides revealing information about family interactions in a two-story Greek house.*

Now, first of all, gentlemen [of the jury], I must explain that I have a small house which is divided into two—the men's quarters and the women's—each having the same [amount of] space, the women upstairs and the men downstairs. After the birth of my child, his mother nursed him; but I did not want her to run the risk of going downstairs every time she had to give him a bath [because the stairs were very steep], so I myself took over the upper story, and let the women have the ground floor. And so it came about that . . . it was quite customary for my wife often to go downstairs and sleep with the child, so that she could give him the breast and stop him from crying.

Sitting Rooms, Kitchens, and Bathrooms

In general, the upper floor in two-story Greek homes was not simply where the women had their quarters. Most or all of the bedrooms were upstairs, including any rooms or attic space allotted to slaves. With occasional exceptions, the bedrooms were tiny cubicles barely large enough to accommodate a single bed and a few personal belongings.

The rooms on the ground floor were mostly larger. Their functions were fairly standard, with some variation from house to house. Many townhouses had an exedra, a sitting area with one or perhaps two sides open to the inner court to take advantage of fresh air and natural light. The opening between the exedra and courtyard was sometimes articulated by a small colonnade (row of columns); these columns, usually no more than three or four in number, were most often made of wood, as the fine marble used for temple colonnades was too expensive for the average family dwelling.

Until the beginning of the mid–fifth century B.C., most Greek homes apparently did not have formal kitchens. Cooking was done either in a brazier—a metal container for burning wood or charcoal, which people set up in the courtyard—or on a stone-lined hearth located in a central combination

This primitive, cluttered kitchen in a Greek monastery (built in medieval times) likely resembles a typical kitchen in an ancient Greek house.

living and workroom. In contrast, the houses at Olynthus, which were built in the later fifth and early fourth centuries B.C., did have small kitchens located off the main room. These kitchens were evidently used for food preparation and likely had storage bins for fruit, bread, and kitchenware. Cooking indoors required some means of allowing smoke to vent. In the average home, this was accomplished by using a pole to push open a pre-loosened roofing tile just before lighting the fire. In more well-to-do houses, small conduits made of baked clay and mounted near the ceiling carried the smoke away.

Some homes, especially the poorest and smallest, did not have bathrooms. In many others the bathroom was simply a closet-size space affording some privacy but without a formal toilet or other plumbing facilities. In such situations, waste was collected in chamber pots, which people emptied by hand into ditches, cesspools, or sewers outside. (In the fifth century B.C., Athens relied on cesspools, or underground pits; in the following century, it had a public sewer system.) Other houses did have more formal bathrooms with toilets. The ones at Olynthus were located beside the main hearth room in order to take advantage of the residual heat. A surprisingly modern-shaped toilet, made of terra-cotta (baked clay), was found in the remains of an Olynthian house. The wastes from the toilet drained into terra-cotta conduits that led to the city's sewers.

Some bathrooms contained tubs for bathing. Such a tub was slightly smaller than a modern version and was made of terracotta. The usual custom was to fill the tub using buckets, work done by slaves in those households that could afford to keep slaves. When the bath was over, the water drained to the outside through a terra-cotta channel recessed in the floor. Most bathrooms also had a basin, which rested on a small table, for washing the hands and face. If one wanted a shower, at least by the early fourth century B.C. one could go to a communal version in a local gymnasium. A painting on a surviving vase from that period shows some men standing beneath showerheads shaped like the faces of lions and boars, through which piped-in water sprays down.

Other Common Rooms

Rooms with several other functions have been identified in the surviving remains of Greek townhouses. Sometimes a small dining room adjoined the kitchen or the main hearth room. This eating area was pre-sumably used by any and all family members.

By contrast, in many Greek houses, even of moderate size, the male head of the household had his own, exclusive dining chamber—the *andron*. (The women of the house were not allowed in or near this room when it was in use.) Here, he hosted banquets and entertained his male guests in after-dinner parties called symposia. During the preliminary meal, usually served by slaves, the men reclined on couches. Because the host wanted to impress his guests, the *andron* was often the most finely decorated room in the house. In several of the excavated Olynthian houses, a narrow raised platform on which the couches rested ran around the room's perimeter. The square-shaped floor space in the center of the chamber was often ornamented with mosaics made of colored pebbles. And

Greek men recline on couches at a party held in their host's andron, *or exclusive dining chamber. This was often the home's most elegantly decorated room.*

the walls were either painted in bright colors (most often red) or bore paintings.

We know what went on at the parties held in these special dining rooms because several ancient writers describe symposia. The highlight seems to have been the after-dinner drinking, which could and often did result in drunkenness. In one of his more famous dialogues, appropriately titled *Symposium,* Plato describes a group of Athenian men, including his mentor, Socrates, who meet in the *andron* of the poet Agathon. Suffering hangovers from drinking too much the night before, they decide to drink more moderately in this session. "When Socrates had settled himself," Plato writes,

and had his dinner like the rest, we poured libations [small amounts of wine intended to appease a god] and sang a hymn to the god . . . and then betook ourselves to drinking. At this point, Pausanias began as follows: "Come now, sirs, what will be the least rigorous rule to make about drinking? I don't mind telling you that yesterday's bout has left me in a very poor

Courtesans entertain guests during an after-dinner party known as a symposium in this scene painted on an ancient bowl.

way." . . . "You are quite right, Pausanias," said Aristophanes. . . . "I am one of those who were pretty well soaked yesterday." . . . After this, everyone agreed that the present party should not be pushed to the point of drunkenness.[9]

In addition to drinking, symposia frequently featured storytelling, riddles and word games, singing songs, and playing games. Those hosts who could afford it also brought in outside entertainers. These included *hetairai*, high-class, highly educated prostitutes who engaged the men in conversation as well as sexual activity. Also common were musicians, dancers, and acrobats. In his own work titled *Symposium*, Xenophon describes such entertainers at a party:

> When the table had been removed and they had poured libations . . . a Syracusan [a native of the Greek city of Syracuse, on the Italian island of Sicily] came to provide entertainment. He had with him a girl who was an expert pipe [flute] player, another who was an acrobatic dancer, and a very attractive boy who both played the lyre [a small harp] and danced extremely well.[10]

A few townhouses had other specialized rooms, notably factory-like workrooms, which suggests that these homes belonged to artisans and manufacturers. ("Factories" in ancient Greece usually consisted of a small group of people doing

A potter decorates a large ceramic pot in a busy workroom.

skilled manual labor in one or more workrooms.) Excavations in Athens's ancient marketplace have revealed the remains of small houses of potters and metalsmiths who plied their trades at home in modest workrooms. Such a situation is also known from surviving literature. Before he became a speechwriter and orator, Lysias, along with his brother, Polemarchus, operated a shield-making shop in Athens; their workrooms seem to have been attached to their living quarters. Lysias later wrote a speech titled *Against Eratosthenes*, in which he described how, during a rare instance when tyrants controlled the city, government agents entered the house. These men killed

Polemarchus, then arrested Lysias, who was entertaining guests in the *andron*. At the same time, the intruders went to the nearby workrooms, where the brothers' slaves were making shields, and closed down the operation.

Common Contents of Homes

The workrooms in Lysias's house and the homes of other artisans were likely cluttered with all manner of materials. In contrast, the furniture, decorations, and other contents of most of the rooms of the average Greek house were rather spare compared to the typical modern home. In regards to walls and floors, evidence from Olynthus shows that, with the exception of the *andron,* walls of ordinary homes were covered with a plain coating of plaster. A few well-to-do homes could afford frescoes (paintings done on wet plaster) and/or hanging tapestries made of embroidered cloth. Better-off families could also afford to install mosaic tiles and handmade rugs on the floors of some rooms.

Most furniture was utilitarian—made strictly for everyday use rather than ornamentation. Beds and couches consisted of a simple wooden frame covered by a thin mattress and pillows, both stuffed with animal fur or feathers. Bedspreads, like rugs, were hand woven and were sometimes dyed in bright colors. Tables (both square- and oval-shaped), chairs, stools, and benches were generally made of wood and were simple in design. Also fashioned from wood were various storage chests and boxes, which rested in many parts of the house since there were no closets or wall cabinets, common features of modern homes. Pottery and bronze containers were also used for storage as well as for cooking and serving meals. Only rarely did Greek houses have interior doors that could be closed and locked; instead, it was most common to hang curtains in the doorways.

By modern standards, the methods of lighting and heating ancient Greek homes were rather primitive. Oil lamps (small shallow vessels that burned wicks fueled by olive oil) and candles (often set in a multiple-candle holder called a candelabra) were the chief lighting devices. (Torches were used mainly for outdoor lighting.) This made reading and other close work difficult at night. It also gave rise to the familiar phrase "burning the midnight oil," a reference to diligent nighttime studies. Heat came from the household hearth and from the braziers used for cooking, many of which were small and portable to make it easier to move them from room to room. On the coolest nights, however, one's best option for staying warm was to huddle with a spouse, sibling, or friend beneath generous layers of bedspreads.

Residential Water Supplies

As in all ages and places, Greek homes could not operate without a ready and reliable water supply. The most common source of freshwater was a well, which could be dug either in the country or the city. (In the cities, some people managed to dig wells in their own courtyards, though these may have been exceptional.) In his biography of the sixth-century B.C. Athenian lawgiver Solon, Plutarch tells how the Athenians relied on wells because there were few rivers and mountain springs in Attica, one of the drier portions of Greece. Cisterns were also prevalent. A cistern is a basin or tank that catches and stores rainwater. Both wells and underground cisterns were usually equipped with stone or terra-cotta lids to keep people and animals from falling in. If the well or cistern was outside the house, those who could afford it installed baked clay pipes to bring the water in; most people, however, resorted to lugging it in buckets.

In those parts of Greece where rainfall, springs, and small rivers were more plentiful, fountain houses were a common source of water for homes. A fountain house was a small building most often erected beside a stream. Water flowed from the stream into stone settling tanks inside, and from the tanks to bronze spouts mounted on an outer wall. People who lived in the surrounding houses filled their buckets from these spouts. Because they were public buildings, fountain houses were usually handsomely decorated and often looked like miniature temples. In his renowned travel guide, the second-century A.D. Greek writer Pausanias mentioned a fountain house in Megara, west of Athens, that was "worth seeing for its size and ornament and the number of columns."[11]

Not all fountain houses were fed by streams. Some received their water from aqueducts, stone channels that carried water from mountain lakes and streams to inhabited regions. An example from the Classical Age has been discovered at Olynthus; it brought the city water from the hills several miles away. However, this was exceptional,

This room in a modern Greek villa was designed to capture the simple, sparsely decorated look of the typical bedchamber in ancient Greece.

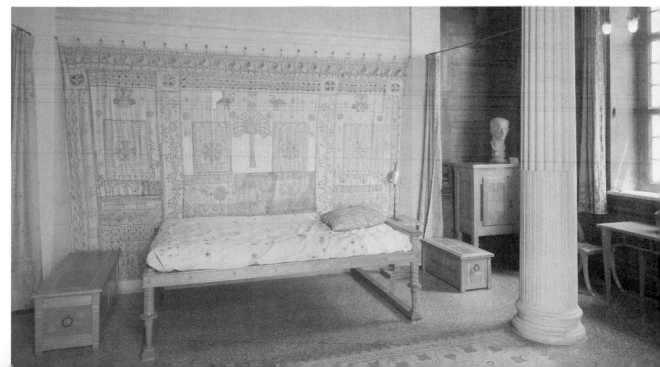

Freshwater for Everyone

All ancient Greek households required access to freshwater, and sometimes it was necessary for the local government to ensure such access for everyone in the community. In his biography of the Athenian law-giver Solon, Plutarch gives this account (from Ian Scott-Kilvert's translation in The Rise and Fall of Athens *) of Solon's efforts to see that everyone in the Athenian territory of Attica had the water they needed.*

Attica cannot rely for her water upon rivers that flow all the year round, or upon lakes or abundant springs, but most of it comes from artificial wells. Solon therefore made a law that wherever there was a public well within a distance of half a mile, everyone [living nearby] should use that, but if the distance was greater they should dig one for themselves. But if, after digging to a depth of ten fathoms on their own land they still could not strike water, they were allowed to fill a vessel of six gallons twice a day at their neighbor's well, for Solon thought it his duty to help those in real need, but not to encourage the idle.

Some ancient Greek houses had wells like this one in a modern Greek home.

for the Greeks built few aqueducts during and before this era, partly because they were so expensive. More importantly, the political situation among the disunited and squabbling city-states discouraged such projects. Erecting water channels across miles of countryside, Wycherley points out, is "unreliable for a city which is frequently at war with its neighbors and from time to time closely besieged."[12] Later, when Rome administered the Greeks and kept the peace, numerous aqueducts were constructed across Greece. And from the fountain houses these channels fed, families drew the life-giving water needed to sustain their private domestic domains.

Chapter

2

The Family: Men's vs. Women's Roles

I n ancient Greece, as remains true today, the home was the abode of the family, or *oikos* (EE-kos). Most Greek families were extended, which meant that it was not unusual to have grandparents, married siblings, in-laws, and cousins living in the same house with the father, mother, and their own children. More importantly, the family was invariably patriarchal, or male-dominated, which reflected the political and legal superiority of men in society in general. In Athens, for example, male citizens were designated *politai*, meaning "citizens with political rights." They could attend meetings of the Assembly (the citizen body that voted leaders into office and debated and passed state legislation); hold public office; sue someone in court or sit on a jury;

and serve in the military. In contrast, female citizens were *astai*, or "citizens without political rights." An *aste* could not vote, hold office, or take a case to court (although she did have the civic rights to take part in and benefit from the community's religious and economic institutions).

Because this male dominance existed at all levels of society, including the family, the husband (or grown son, uncle, or other male relative if the husband was deceased) was the head of the household. Usually his word was law. He set and enforced the rules, distributed money to family members, hired servants or bought slaves, and arranged for his children's education. Accordingly, his wife, children, other live-in relatives, and slaves were expected to do as he said and perform their respective household duties.

In practice, however, in most cases the home was not the principal domain of Greek men. Outside of eating and sleeping there, the vast majority of men actually spent little time in their homes. Indeed, the bulk of a man's day was devoted to outside activities—working in the fields, vineyards, or marketplace, fulfilling military duties, or spending time in the law courts, the gymnasium, and so on. In his *Oeconomicus*, sometimes translated as the *Householder*, Xenophon creates a character named Ischomachus, portrayed as a typical Athenian gentleman. Ischomachus says, "I don't spend any time at all indoors. My wife is perfectly capable of managing my household by herself." [13]

This comment reveals that in reality a Greek wife (or mother or other female relative if the head of the household was not married) actually ran the household on a day-to-day basis. With few exceptions, women spent most of their time in the home, the exact opposite of their menfolk. And within the home, women's roles and responsibilities were as important to the household's success as their husbands' and fathers' were to the success of the larger community. Xenophon probably spoke for most Greek men when he recognized that each gender had its specialized duties:

Since both of these domains—indoor and outdoor—require work and attention, then God, as I see it, directly made women's nature suitable for the indoor

These drawings of Greek women came from surviving vase paintings. In the Classical Age, Athenian women spent most of their time at home.

jobs and tasks, and man's nature suitable for the outdoor ones. . . . We must recognize what God has assigned to each of us, and try our hardest to carry through our respective responsibilities. [14]

Because the responsibilities of the home fell mainly on women, their duties, roles, and struggles to maintain domestic order and harmony were the predominant themes of Greek family life.

Women's Restrictions and Duties

To ensure that Greek women fulfilled these duties and roles to their utmost (and also to maintain the male-dominated status quo), Greek men closely regulated and restricted women. Evidence suggests that most women enjoyed more rights and freedoms in the Archaic Age, the era preceding the Classical period; but in late Archaic times, community leaders (who were all men) began passing laws that strictly controlled women's social and sexual behavior and limited what they could own or inherit.

One restriction on Athenian women involved segregating them from men to some degree much of the time. This was one of the main reasons that many women spent so much time at home. The main rationale was not so much to keep women secluded but rather to prevent respectable wives, mothers, and daughters from conversing with unrelated males, which was viewed as offensive and ominous. Husbands and fathers were very preoccupied with their wives' and daughters' chastity and marital

fidelity. And men outside the family unit were seen as potentially corruptive influences that threatened the stability of the *oikos.* For these reasons, the family men or slaves usually did the shopping; this eliminated the chance of a wife or daughter meeting strange men in the marketplace. Also, when a respectable woman did leave the house, a male relative or family slave customarily accompanied her.

This perceived need to keep the family women segregated from nonfamilial men often restricted women's mobility in the home as well. When the head of the household was having a symposium or other gathering attended by male friends, his wife, daughters, mother, and sisters were not allowed to be seen by, let alone to mix with, the guests. At such times, the ladies of the house retired to the *gynaeceum,* or "women's quarters," located in the back of the house or upstairs. There, they spun thread, wove fabric, or visited with female guests until the male visitors were gone. The Roman writer Cornelius Nepos, who visited Athens not long after the Classical Age, found such segregation of women odd and compared it unfavorably to the custom in his own society:

Many actions are seemly according to our [i.e., the Roman] code, which the Greeks look upon as shameful. For instance, what Roman would blush to take his wife to a dinner-party? What matron does not frequent the front rooms of her dwelling and show herself in public? But it is very different in

This drawing exaggerates the appearance of the gynaeceum, *or "women's quarters." In reality, such rooms were usually small and far less opulent.*

[Athens]; for there a woman is not admitted to a dinner-party, unless relatives only are present, and she keeps to the more retired part of the house called "the women's apartment," to which no man has access who is not near of kin. [15]

The rest of the time, the family women had the run of the house and performed their many and varied duties. In addition to spinning and weaving, these included helping to prepare meals, making shopping lists for the men and slaves, overseeing the children and servants, paying the bills, cleaning, and in general keeping the home well organized. Xenophon had Ischomachus tell his young wife:

You must receive the produce that is brought in from outside and distribute as much of it as needs dispensing. . . . When wool is brought in to you, you must try to make certain that those who need clothes get them. And you must try to ensure that the grain is made into edible provisions. . . . When any servant is ill, you must make sure that he is thoroughly looked after.[16]

Thus, although the husband or father set the rules and provided the money to support the household, the wife or mother and her female kin, if any, kept that household running smoothly.

Betrothal and Marriage

One aspect of family life in which both men and women played important and nearly equal roles was getting married. Most mar-

riages in Athens, and presumably the vast majority of other Greek states, were arranged by fathers or other male family members. And it was not unusual for a young bride and groom barely to know each other before their wedding night. Therefore, many men, along with almost all women, had little or no say in choosing a spouse. Also, the social customs surrounding marriage did not take into account falling in love and other personal feelings. It was not that romantic love, as it is known today, did not exist. Some evidence suggests that it did but that it was either uncommon, discouraged, not taken seriously by most people, or all of these.

A Greek bride prepares for her wedding in this drawing based on a vase painting. Such celebrations were long, elaborate, and festive.

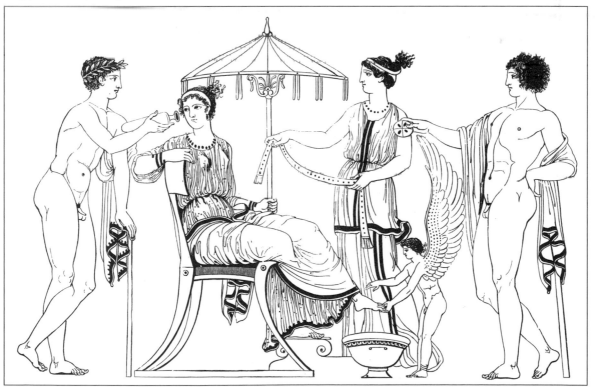

Not only were marriages mainly arranged beforehand, but a young man or woman sometimes found that he or she had been paired with a relative. Intimate relationships between parents and children or brother and sister from the same mother were viewed as incest and a taboo. (This is clear from the Athenian playwright Sophocles' great drama *Oedipus the King,* in which the title character's inadvertent marriage to his mother is treated as a terrible abomination.) However, it was acceptable for a half brother to marry his sister, and unions between male and female cousins and uncles and nieces were not uncommon. Scholars suspect that one reason for this custom was to help reinforce and perpetuate family ties; it also kept any dowry monies within the immediate family.

The marriage dowry (the money provided by the bride's father for her maintenance) was part of the legal arrangement accompanying a marriage. The deal was always made by the father and/or other leading men in the family. The bride-to-be's father (or brother, uncle, or grown son if the father was dead) was her *kyrios,* or legal guardian, and her prospective husband became her *kyrios* when the marriage took place. These parties negotiated the details of the dowry at a formal betrothal (*engue*), which most often occurred in front of witnesses. In her book about ancient Greek women, scholar Sue Blundell describes the dowry and its importance:

Its principal component was generally a sum of money, but furniture and other moveable goods might also be included. Land might also be an element, but this would not have been common, since most men would want to keep their estates intact for their sons. . . . A large dowry, as well as being an eloquent expression of a man's wealth and social status, was undoubtedly useful in attracting eligible suitors. . . . On divorce, [the husband] was obliged to return the dowry to his wife's original *kyrios.*[17]

The social implications of dowries were sometimes profound. For example, fathers who were not wealthy were unlikely to raise more daughters than they could afford to supply dowries for. As a result, some fathers exposed (left outside to die) one or more of the infant girls born to their wives. Also, a man who was heavily in debt might view marriage to a woman with a substantial dowry as a solution to his money troubles. This could have serious consequences later if he squandered the dowry money and then, when he wanted a divorce, could not pay it back.

Following the betrothal, the families proceeded with plans for the wedding celebration (*gamos*). No complete descriptions of the ceremony itself have survived. However, noted classical scholar Robert Flaceliere gives this credible scenario of an Athenian wedding, pieced together from various literary and other sources:

The sequence of ceremonies began on the evening before the bride's change of abode. First, a sacrifice was offered

Ancient Greek Dowries

An initial exchange of money or other valuables was one of the most important aspects of marriage in ancient Greece. In the Archaic Age (ca. 800–500 B.C.), and probably long before, this had taken the form of "bride wealth," consisting of gifts given by the groom to the bride's father. By the end of Archaic times, however, this custom had been largely replaced by one in which the property exchanged was a dowry (*proix*)—money or other valuables the bride's father provided for her financial support. In effect, a dowry was an indirect way for a father to leave property to his daughter without allocating her the family land, which was reserved for his sons. The money making up the dowry was supposed to remain intact throughout her life and be used primarily for her maintenance. Her husband could use the principal—the original sum—any way he liked. But if he did, he had to pay interest on the amount he used at the high rate of 18 percent. Also, if the couple divorced, the husband had to return the entire principal of the dowry to his ex-wife's father or other guardian or else pay interest, once again at 18 percent, until he did so.

up to those gods and goddesses who protected the marriage bed. . . . The bride offered up her toys, and all other objects associated with her childhood. . . . On the day of the wedding, the houses of both the bride and groom were decorated with garlands made from olive and laurel leaves, and there was a sacrifice and banquet at the house of the bride's father. The bride herself was present at this feast, veiled and wearing her finest clothes. . . . This wedding-feast included certain traditional dishes, such as sesame cakes, a symbolic guarantee of fertility. . . . At last, towards evening, the [wedding] procession formed up to convey the bride to her new home. . . . Bride and bridegroom were carried . . . [in] a wagon drawn by mules or oxen, with a friend of the bridegroom's to drive it. . . . Relatives and friends [followed] on foot, lit by flaring torches. During the procession the marriage hymn was sung. . . . When they reached the door of the bridegroom's house, his father and mother were waiting there. . . . Nuts and dried figs were showered on the bride. . . . The couple [then] proceeded straight to the bridal chamber . . . while the rest of the company sang some nuptial hymn at the tops of their voices . . . to scare away evil spirits.[18]

Divorce and Adultery

In Athens and most other Greek states, as remains the case in modern Western countries, bad marriages could be remedied by divorce. Both men and women could initiate the procedure, though the laws involved were heavily weighted in favor of men. A man who wanted a divorce could simply order his wife out of the house, in which case she usually returned to the guardianship of her father, brother, or another male relative. In contrast, a woman who wanted a divorce had to get a male relative (or some other male citizen) to ask for legal permission from a high-ranking civil official called an archon. There was still another kind of divorce in Athens, which the wife's father could initiate if he suspected her husband was abusing her or misusing her dowry. In most divorces, the husband got custody of the children, no surprise in a society so closely controlled by men.

One of the chief causes of divorce was adultery (*moicheia*). It was viewed as a very serious offense because it brought the legitimacy of the couple's children into doubt and shamed the entire family. A woman who committed adultery was disgraced, sometimes for the rest of her life, which made it difficult for her to find a second husband.

On the other hand, the man involved in an adulterous affair often faced even more severe penalties. This was because society viewed adultery as a situation in which a man knowingly corrupted or seduced a woman, who was seen as the victim. The seducer could be prosecuted or even killed by her male relatives. According to an ancient Athenian law that still existed in Classical times, a husband who caught another man with his wife was allowed to slay the offender on the spot. The one proviso was that, if someone could prove that he had some other motive for the killing, he could be prosecuted for murder.

For instance, in the earlier mentioned case of the Athenian Euphiletus, for whom Lysias wrote the speech for the defense, Euphiletus killed a man he had caught in bed with his wife. The man's relatives then accused him of plotting the whole situation leading up to the killing and prosecuted him on a charge of murder. The outcome of the case is unknown. But if Euphiletus was found guilty, he might have received the death penalty.

Spartan Family Life

Male-female relationships, marriage, and home life in other parts of the ancient Greek world were likely at least similar to those in Athens. There were a few exceptions, however, the most famous, both then and now, being Sparta. The main reason that Spartan life was so different from the norm was that during the Archaic Age Sparta adopted a strict, regimented military-social system known as the *agoge* (uh-GO-gee). Thereafter, every aspect of Spartan life, including home life, contributed to producing machinelike soldiers for the army.

One of the most striking aspects of this system was that it made Spartan men largely absentee husbands and fathers. As boys,

A Male View of Women's Worth

Most ancient Greek men felt that if a woman performed her household duties faithfully, she would prove her worth as a wife and citizen and had a chance to achieve happiness. In Xenophon's Householder *(in Tredennick's and Waterfield's* Conversations with Socrates *) the character Ischomachus tells his young wife:*

A funerary stele (stone marker) shows a dutiful Greek wife with her husband and son.

You will have to stay indoors and send out the servants who have outside jobs, and oversee those with indoor jobs. You must receive the produce that is brought in from outside and distribute as much of it as needs dispensing; but . . . you must look ahead and make sure that the outgoings [moneys to pay the bills] assigned for the year are not dispensed in a month. When wool is brought in to you, you must try to make certain that those who need clothes get them. And you must try to ensure that the grain is made into edible provisions. . . . When any servant is ill, you must make sure that he is thoroughly looked after. . . . Some of your specific responsibilities will be gratifying, such as getting a servant who is ignorant of spinning, teaching it to her, and doubling her value to you. . . . And the most gratifying thing of all will be if you turn out to be better than me, and make me your servant. . . . As you grow older, you will have more standing in the household, in proportion to the increase in your value to me as a partner and to our children as a protector of the home. For it is virtue rather than the physical beauty of youth that increases true goodness in human life.

they were forced to leave home at the age of seven. And until they were thirty, they had to eat and sleep in military barracks with other males and were not permitted to live with their wives and children. Moreover, even the older married men were often absent from the home—either training for or fighting in wars, hunting, or engaging in politics. The result, Blundell points out, was that a Spartan man had much less authority and personal say in family life than his Athenian counterpart. "There can be little doubt," she writes,

that one effect of undermining the father's role would have been to enhance that of the mother, who by the time her husband moved into the family home would have established her pre-eminence there. . . . [The] rad-

ical separation of the public and private spheres . . . would have ensured that female domestic power was accepted and possibly even officially encouraged.[19]

Indeed, with the father and sons absent most of the time, a Spartan home was largely a female environment populated by mother, daughters, and other women. This naturally fostered a good deal of independence and assertiveness among Spartan women. Evidence shows that they enjoyed numerous rights and privileges that many other Greek women did not. It appears, for example, that they did not merely manage the household, as women in Athens did, but actually made the rules and enforced them. Furthermore, the Spartans had more slaves than the Athenians and other Greeks, which

Spartan men were forced to undergo a vigorous physical education. Spartan life was dominated by a rigid system of military training.

meant that Spartan women had to do very little menial labor, either inside or outside the home. This freed them to pursue other activities, including athletic training, a situation rarely seen in other Greek states.

Neither were Spartan women confined in the home or denied contact and conversations with nonfamilial men. With minor exceptions, a female Spartan could appear in public whenever she pleased. Spartan women were also outspoken and did not hesitate to comment on politics or give advice to the men who ran state affairs. In his biography of a Spartan leader named Agis, Plutarch remarks that "Spartan men were always subject to their wives and allowed them to interfere in affairs of state more than they themselves did in private ones."[20]

It must not be inferred from this independent and bold behavior that Spartan women had more authority in society than the men. Men still held all the positions of real power, and Spartan women had no more political rights than Athenian women did. Spartan men also enjoyed a stronger position in two important aspects of family and home life—inheritance and landownership. A Spartan woman's share of the family inheritance was only half that of her brother. Still, she was much better off in this respect than women in other Greek states, since she could inherit land and other family property directly. (By contrast, an Athenian heiress had to marry a male relative to ensure that she gained access to her legacy.) Under these unusually liberal conditions, female Spartans eventually gained control of large amounts of land. According to the conservative Athenian Aristotle, who felt that Spartan women enjoyed too much freedom, they owned two-fifths of the land in Sparta by the mid–fourth century B.C.

A Strange Nocturnal Ritual

No discussion of Spartan home life would be complete without considering the highly unusual customs of Spartan courting and marriage. According to Plutarch, Spartan girls paraded nude in public processions and athletic games partly to attract the attentions of young men. Once a relationship was formed and the two families consented to a marriage, a strange nocturnal ritual took place, one consistent with the militaristic customs of the *agoge*. "The custom," Plutarch explains,

was to capture women for marriage. . . . The so-called "bridesmaid" took charge of the captured girl. She first shaved her head to the scalp, then dressed her in a man's cloak and sandals, and laid her down alone on a mattress in the dark. The bridegroom—who was not drunk and thus not impotent, but was sober as always—first had dinner in the messes [i.e., with his male comrades], then would slip in, undo her belt, lift her and carry her to the bed. After spending only a short time with her, he would depart discreetly so as to sleep wherever he usually did along with the other young men. And this continued to be his practice thereafter. . . . He would warily visit his bride in secret . . . apprehensive in case someone in the house might notice him. His bride at the same time devised schemes and helped to plan how they might meet each other unobserved at suitable moments. It was not just for a short period that young men would do this, but for long enough that some might even have children before they saw their own wives in daylight.[21]

Changing the Family Dynamic

Spartan society, with its odd male-female relationships and unique domestic situa-

tions, remained largely aloof from the Greek mainstream, even after the conquests of Alexander the Great brought the Classical Age to a close. Most other Greek states felt the winds of change, however. The Hellenistic Age witnessed the growth of large Greek kingdoms in the Aegean and Near Eastern spheres. And many Greeks, including civil servants, artisans, merchants, and especially soldier-farmers, migrated from the old city-states to the larger monarchies. Vast new economic and cultural opportunities stimulated expanded social horizons in which many (but certainly not all) people began to redefine

A Young Woman Stands Up to Her Father

In Hellenistic times, some Greek women were less afraid to stand up to their fathers and other male authorities. In this fragment from an anonymous comic play (quoted in Lefkowitz's and Fant's Women's Life in Ancient Greece and Rome*), an Athenian maid boldly asserts herself when her father tries to dissolve her marriage and force her to marry a richer man:*

Father, you ought to be making the speech that I am now making, because you ought to have more sense than I have. . . . There is a covenant between man and wife; he must love her, always, until the end, and she must never cease to do what gives her husband pleasure. He was all that I wished with regard to me, and my pleasure is his pleasure. But suppose he is satisfactory as far as I am concerned but is bankrupt. . . . Where does so much money exist, father, that having it can give me more pleasure than my husband can? How can it be just or honorable that I should take a share of any good things he has, but take no share in his poverty? . . . When I was a young girl, you had to find a husband [for] me, when the choice was yours. But once you had given me to a husband, from that moment this responsibility belonged to me, naturally, because if I make a mistake in judgment, it's my own life that I shall ruin.

their worldviews, including their personal relationships.

Although home life remained the same as before in a number of ways, these changes subtly but profoundly transformed the family dynamic. Both male and female attitudes were affected. The decline in status of small city-states governed largely by local citizens and the rise of big monarchies altered the political and social position of many men. In the large Greek kingdoms, in which the kings made the laws, most men no longer had a say in government; they also enjoyed fewer civic rights and privileges. This had two significant effects. First, a number of men began to focus more on private life, including the family, than on communal concerns. This meant that more husbands helped their wives run the household and more fathers spent more time with their children. Second, these same men experienced a narrowing of the gap in privileges that had long existed between men and women. This gave more and more men an appreciation for what it felt like to be second-class citizens; and accordingly, they were more willing to accord their wives and daughters certain privileges that they had long been denied.

Many Hellenistic women therefore experienced small but significant gains in status and rights. Most were still excluded from political life, yet their increased economic clout helped make up for it. Many Greek women in the large kingdoms were allowed to grant and receive loans; to buy and sell land, slaves, and other property; to inherit property directly from their fathers

Women appear with their husbands in public during Hellenistic times.

and to bequeath that same property to their children; and to make their own marriage contracts (although in many places they still needed the consent of their fathers or other guardians). Also, large numbers of women were less segregated than before, and in some places respectable women could leave the house, shop, and engage in public conversations without a male escort.

Thus, at the same time that many men endured diminished social status, many women enjoyed the opposite. Ancient Greek men and women never achieved true equality, to be sure. But the social and legal gap between them narrowed enough in Hellenistic times to make family life a more shared and perhaps a more fruitful experience for many couples.

The Family: Children and Education

Most modern-day parents look forward to having children because they want to experience the joys and challenges of parenthood. Some feel that they cannot be "complete" human beings without the experience of having children, and a few become parents because of the expectations and subtle pressures of family, friends, and society in general.

Of these motivations, the only one that was common in ancient Greece was the last. Familial pressure to have children was likely strong because tradition made it the duty of both men and women to see that the family line did not die out. It was especially important to have a son since property and inheritance laws were written by and largely to accommodate the needs of men. Another

traditional duty was to ensure that the community was perpetuated. Most Greek city-states were small, with only a few thousand citizens, and if these people did not reproduce themselves, there was a danger that the state might not have the human resources to defend itself. Here, too, having sons was a priority because men did the fighting.

For these and other reasons, most of the relatives and friends of a pregnant woman hoped the baby was a boy. If it was not, the father or other male head of the household sometimes decided that the female infant should be exposed. Baby boys were occasionally exposed, too, especially if they were physically deformed in some way. But as Mark Golden, an authority on Greek children, points out, daughters were probably refused admission to the family and exposed more frequently than sons, [which was] a father's decision. . . . Archaic and early Classical Athenian tombs that identify themselves [through inscriptions] as sons' outnumber those of daughters by about five to one.[22]

Thus, one common modern attitude toward having children—that all babies will be welcome, loved, and cared for, regardless of gender or physical attributes—did not exist in ancient Greece. Where new babies were concerned, the immediate needs of the family and society usually took precedence over personal feelings and humanitarian ideals.

The question of whether an infant should live or die was only the first of many important issues and customs surrounding children and childhood in ancient Greece. Childbirth was itself a serious matter because the incidence of babies and mothers dying in the process was much higher than it is today. Other issues affecting children included adoption, societal perceptions of children, children's premature deaths, child labor, and, perhaps most important all, the education of both boys and girls.

Childbirth and Infant Mortality

Just as in modern society, in ancient Greece not all pregnancies were carried to full term and delivery. Some expectant mothers miscarried. Or a husband might choose to abort the fetus because he felt the family could not afford to raise another child. The beliefs and practices surrounding abortion in ancient Greece are somewhat unclear. Apparently there were no laws against it. Yet there may have been some religious sanctions against performing an abortion after the fetus had attained a certain level of development. Plato and Aristotle had no

This sculpture shows a small family unit, including a child.

objections to abortion; and Aristotle even recommended it as a means of restricting population growth. Evidently most abortions were accomplished by subjecting the woman to vigorous physical activity (shaking and jumping up and down), or the use of drugs to induce premature delivery. Surgical procedures like those common today were probably rare because of the extreme risks involved.

A pregnant woman who did carry her baby to full term almost always gave birth in her home, either in her bedroom or in the women's quarters, if the house was so equipped. The common custom was to utilize a midwife (*maia*), who was assisted by the expectant mother's female relatives. Usually, the woman gave birth seated upright on a birthing stool. But evidence suggests that some women delivered while

A mother nurses her child in this painting inspired by an ancient vase. Unless they were physically unable to do so, ancient Greek women breast-fed their babies.

Tending to Infants

It is evident that ancient Greek infants were well cared for from this excerpt from a speech by a nurse in the Athenian dramatist Aeschylus's play The Libation Bearers *(in Richmond Lattimore's translation of the Oresteia trilogy).*

Darling Orestes! I wore out my life for him. I took him from his mother, brought him up. There were times when he screamed at night and woke me from my rest; I had to do many hard tasks. . . . A baby is like a beast; it does not think but you have to nurse it . . . the way it wants. For the child still in swaddling clothes cannot tell us if he is hungry or thirsty, [or] if he needs to [pee]. Children's young insides are a law unto themselves.

lying on their backs. Sometimes potent combinations of herbs were administered to speed up delivery or induce labor. This might also be accomplished by shaking the woman forcefully. "At the moment of birth," Sue Blundell writes, "the mother's helpers uttered a ritual cry of joy." And after the delivery, "mother and child were given a ritual bath,"[23] because the prevailing belief was that the process of childbirth polluted (religiously tainted) them until the bath symbolically cleansed them.

Soon after the birth, the father or another male relative decided whether the child would be kept and reared. If the decision was affirmative, the parents announced the birth to the community by pinning an olive stem to the door if it was a boy or a piece of wool if it was a girl. The new mother also visited a shrine to thank a friendly goddess for watching over her and her newborn.

(The deities involved were usually either Artemis, who was believed to help expectant mothers, or Ilithyia, the goddess of childbirth.)

Not surprisingly, more somber religious rituals took place when women died in childbirth. The proportion of pregnant Greek women who met this unfortunate end is unknown, but most modern scholars think 10 to 20 percent is probable. Such deaths were likely partly attributable to the high proportion of teenage mothers (who even today run a higher risk of complications in pregnancy and birth) as well as widespread ignorance about proper hygiene. Even the minimum figure of 10 percent for maternal mortality is horrendously high by modern standards. In comparison, only one woman in ten thousand (.01 percent) dies in childbirth in the United States today.

Infant mortality rates in ancient Greece were even higher. Mark Golden estimates that as many as 25 to 35 percent of children died in their first year of life (compared with less than 1 percent in the United States today). This means that many Greek women, perhaps the majority, lost at least one child in their lifetimes. Considering this grim reality, some modern scholars suggest that a large proportion of Greek women may have been conditioned not to feel such losses too strongly. Consequently, some scholars infer that maternal love, and perhaps paternal love as well, was not as strong as it is today. This hypothesis is not convincing, however. Surviving sources from ancient Athens contain many references to mothers' anguish at losing children. "The weight of the evidence," Golden says, "seems overwhelmingly to favor the proposition that the Athenians loved their children and grieved for them deeply when they died."[24]

New Members of the Family

If the child survived the birth process and appeared healthy, he or she needed to be formally accepted into the *oikos* and clan (a larger kinship group made up of a number of families who all claimed descent from a common ancestor). In Athens, two postbirth ceremonies celebrated this acceptance. One was the *amphidromia,* which took place on the fifth or seventh day after birth. Relatives made offerings to the gods, and the father carried the child around the family hearth, the home's symbolic center.

Relatives and friends also sent gifts, traditional favorites being octopus and squid. Some children, most often girls, received their names during the *amphidromia,* but most boys were named at a second ceremony, the *decate,* celebrated on the tenth day after birth. This was a festive occasion open to neighbors and other members of the community and highlighted by dancing and eating cake.

If the child being honored was a boy, the parents (especially the father) were satisfied because the family now had a legitimate heir. If, after a number of tries, they produced no male child, it was common to resort to adoption. As noted scholar Alfred Zimmern explains, adoption had more serious legal and social significance in ancient Greece than it does today because a father with no male heir faced what his society viewed as a grave dilemma:

> There was nothing probably in the whole range of life which the Greek dreaded more. No one to tend him in old age, to close his eyes in death and give him ritual burial, to give [away] the daughters in marriage . . . to cherish the memory of the dead and keep alive the institutions that were so dear to him—in a word, to "save the hearth." . . . Such was the sentiment which originated divorce . . . [and] gave rise to the facility and frequency of adoption.[25]

The adoptee (the child being adopted) was almost always a relative, most often a nephew or cousin. After all, the main purpose of adoption was to maintain both the bloodline and the physical property of the immediate family; and to adopt an outsider seemed to work against these goals. Accordingly, in unusual cases in which the adoptee was not kin, other relatives often sued in court and juries usually sided with them and declared the adoptions invalid.

This funerary stele from Athens bears a carving showing three generations of women from one family.

In cases where the parents could not adopt a son or the adoptee died in childhood, the law provided a loophole through which the family's bloodline and property could pass on through a daughter. In Athens, such a young woman was called an *epikleros*, which meant "without property." On the death of her father, she had to marry a male relative, usually either her paternal uncle (her father's brother) or that man's eldest son (her cousin). That way, the deceased father's property remained at least within the extended family.

Children's Activities

Whether born or adopted into the family, Greek children grew up in an atmosphere that most people today would view as bordering on the abusive. It was not simply that corporal punishment, including beatings with wooden rods and leather straps, was accepted and common. The general societal view of children and childhood was more negative than positive, and there was little or no concern with making children happy or developing their self-esteem.

In fact, childhood was not perceived as a blissful, memorable time of life, and adults felt little or no nostalgia for their youth. This stemmed in part from the belief that children lacked proper reasoning powers, courage, or even a moral capacity until they were at least in their teens. Instead, the reasoning went, young children were unpredictable, undisciplined, and potentially destructive beings; so they needed to be closely watched, carefully trained, and, when necessary, harshly disciplined by parents, teachers, and other community members. Following this reasoning, Plato compared children to animals and slaves. "Of all animals" he added,

the boy is the most unmanageable, insomuch as his fountain of reason is not yet regulated. He is the most insidious and . . . insubordinate of animals. And that is why he must be bound with many bridles; in the first place, when he gets away from mothers and nurses, he must be under the management of tutors on account of his childishness and foolishness. . . . Any freeman who comes in his way may punish him . . . if he does anything wrong; and he who . . . does not inflict upon him the punishment he deserves shall incur the greatest disgrace. [26]

On the positive side, young children were allowed to have toys. These included some that are familiar today, such as balls, hoops, tops, yo-yos, and dolls. They also played with miniature carts and chariots.

The ancient Greeks perceived children as a precious community resource. However, children were usually harshly disciplined.

A woman shops for toys for her children in a Greek city in the Hellenistic Age. Because toys were made by hand, each was unique.

Craftsmen manufactured many of these items, yet evidence suggests that some ambitious children made their own versions using whatever materials were easily available. In *Clouds,* by the comic playwright Aristophanes, a father fondly remembers that when his son "was a toddler, he used to build mud-houses, scoop out ships, make carts out of leather, and the loveliest frogs out of pomegranate rind." [27] Children also kept pets. Surviving paintings on vases and cups show boys and girls playing with dogs as well as ducks, weasels, and mice.

Playtime was limited, however, as many parents eventually put their children to work in one capacity or another. The age at which this occurred varied widely from household to household and often depended on the family's financial status, since poorer families often required the help of every available hand to survive. At least by the age of eight, poor children began working, sometimes full time. As young boys, the Athenian playwright Phrynichus spent long hours each day tending sheep, and the Athenian orator Aeschines made ink and cleaned the schoolroom for his father, who was a teacher. Other common tasks relegated to children were running errands, helping the mother and/or slaves clean the house, doing laundry, looking after younger siblings, tending the family's animals, and clearing stones from fields. In addition, potters, metalsmiths, and other artisans frequently made their young sons learn their trades as apprentices. At least in families of modest means, Golden writes,

> Greeks in the Classical period generally regarded sons and daughters in menial occupations as substitutes for slave labor. It is possible that the children of some slave-owning families did chores too, to release slaves for other tasks or as a form of discipline and training. [28]

Educating Young Men

Better-off families (as well as some poorer families that recognized the value of getting a good education) placed more stress on a boy's attending school than on his work at menial tasks, although some boys undoubtedly did both. Even before they were ready for school, young Greek boys learned much about life at home. Parents, grandparents, other relatives, and slaves told them traditional stories. Some of these tales dealt with the past events of their city-state or region or with myths about gods and heroes of distant ages; others were fables, usually populated by talking animals and always ending with some moral lesson.

Already familiarized with these basic facts and lessons, young Athenian boys began attending school at about age seven or eight. Schools in Athens were privately run and paid for mostly by parents, although the government paid for the education of boys whose fathers had died in battle defending the community. The students learned reading and writing from teachers called *grammatistes*. The number of Greeks who learned to read in this or some other manner is unknown, as no one kept records of literacy rates at the time. But evidence suggests that illiteracy was still common in Athens at the start of the fifth century B.C., whereas by the end of that century most adult men could read. This implies that society placed a markedly increased stress on education as the century progressed.

Once a boy could read, he began absorbing the verses of popular poets. According to Plato:

> When the boy has learned his letters . . . they put into his hands the works of great poets, which he reads sitting on a bench at school; in these are contained many pieces of advice, and many tales, and praises and glorification of ancient famous men, which he is required to learn by heart, in order that he may imitate . . . and desire to become like them. [29]

Most important of all were the writings of Homer, the legendary eighth-century B.C. bard whose epic poems, the *Iliad* (about the Trojan War) and the *Odyssey* (describing the adventures of the hero Odysseus), were highly revered by all Greeks. "The Greeks regarded Homer as the educator *par excellence*," says Robert Flaceliere, and teachers drew lessons of a moral and religious nature from his texts for the benefit of their pupils. These lessons might go further . . . [and] take the form of general precepts for life, since in Homer was contained whatever knowledge a man worthy of his name could need. [Homer] ranged over all the various activities of war and peace, the crafts and skills, diplomacy and politics, wisdom, courtesy, courage, [and] men's duties towards their parents and the gods. [30]

Schoolboys also learned to sing and play the lyre from music teachers known as *kitharistes*. Meanwhile, the equivalent of today's gym teachers, which the Greeks called *paidotribes*, supervised the boys in

dancing and athletic events, including running, broad jumping, and throwing the discus and javelin. All the while, the average student was watched closely by his *paidagogos*. As Flaceliere explains:

This was a personal slave-attendant whose business it was to accompany the boy wherever he went, and to teach him good manners. . . . To this end, he was permitted to employ corporal punishment as a means of enforcing obedience, particularly the birch [branch]. It was the *paidagogos* who took the child to school each morning and carried his satchel (containing wax writing-tablets, stylus [quill pen], books, and later both flute and lyre). [31]

Students learn writing and music in this school scene painted on a vase. Schools were privately run institutions supported by parents.

Sparta's School of Hard Knocks

On the whole, education in many other Greek city-states was presumably similar to that in Athens (although some differences undoubtedly existed). The major exception was Sparta. There, because the regimented, militaristic *agoge* penetrated and controlled nearly all aspects of society, the upbringing and education of Spartan boys is best described as a school of hard knocks.

First, Spartan elders examined all male infants and ordered those they saw as too weak to be exposed. Spartan boys who were allowed to live entered state-run schools at age seven. Although they received instruction in basic reading and writing, along with some dancing, poetry, and patriotic songs, the emphasis was on physical endurance and military training. According to Plutarch:

The boys learned to read and write no more than was necessary. Otherwise their whole education was aimed at developing smart obedience, perseverance under stress, and victory in battle. So as they grew older, they intensified their physical training, and got into the habit of cropping their hair, going barefoot, and exercising naked. From the

The Limitations of Illiteracy

The existence and limitations of illiteracy in ancient Greece are well illustrated by the famous story of a meeting between the Athenian politician Aristides, often called "the Just" because of his honesty, and a farmer who could not read or write, as told by Plutarch (in his biography of Aristides, translated by Ian Scott-Kilvert in The Rise and Fall of Athens *).*

The [democratic] institution of ostracism [worked] . . . as follows. Each voter took an *ostrakon*, or [broken] piece of [pottery], [and] wrote on it the name of the citizen he wished to see banished. . . . [State officials] sorted the votes and the man who had the most recorded against his name was . . . exiled for ten years. . . . The story goes that [when Aristides was being ostracized], while the votes were being written down, an illiterate and uncouth rustic handed his piece of [pottery] to Aristides and asked him to write the name of Aristides on it. The latter was astonished and asked the man what harm Aristides had ever done him. "None whatever," was the reply. "I don't even know the fellow, but I'm sick of hearing him called the Just everywhere!" When he heard this, Aristides said nothing, but wrote his name on the *ostrakon* and handed it back.

Like all young Greek men, Spartan youths attended gymnasia, where they participated in wrestling, boxing, discus throwing, and other events.

age of twelve, they never wore a tunic, and were given only one cloak a year. . . . They slept together . . . on mattresses which they made for themselves from the tips of [river] reeds. [32]

During these years, Plutarch writes, the boys were purposely given little to eat so as to encourage them to steal food, whereby they learned "how to pounce skillfully upon those who are asleep or keeping guard carelessly. A boy is beaten or goes hungry if he is caught." [33]

Between the ages of fourteen and twenty, the boys learned about weapons and fighting and took part in drills and mock battles so rigorous that some suffered serious wounds. Each was also expected to stalk and kill at least one agricultural slave as a rite of passage, a practice fully condoned by the state. Any young man who could not measure up to these murderous standards was treated with utter disdain and cruelty. Such youths (as well as Spartan men who ran from battle) were called "tremblers." They had to wear cloaks with colored patches to mark them from the "honorable" Spartans, and they suffered constant mockery, even by members of their own families.

Educating Young Women

Many Greek girls received educations, too, although in general their schooling was almost always less formal and less extensive than that of boys. Athenian girls did not attend formal schools, for instance, but were taught at home by their mothers. Spinning, weaving, sewing, and basic math skills (for doing the family bills) were primary areas of instruction, although mothers, fathers, or educated slaves taught some young women to read and write. Girls were not encouraged to take part in athletics, as boys were.

People who have grown up in modern societies in which both boys and girls attend school may wonder why Athenian and many other Greek girls did not receive formal schooling. First, society did not perceive any compelling need for it. The main form of communication in ancient times was the spoken word, and it was neither a handicap nor a disgrace to be illiterate. Also, women were barred from politics, intellectual pursuits, and most athletic games, in all of which one's performance was enhanced by a good education. Another factor was the widely accepted view that women were intellectually inferior to men. And still another was that many men saw an educated woman as a potential threat to the male-dominated order, in which women were expected to know their place. One old saying drilled into Athenian schoolboys was, "A man who teaches a woman to write should recognize that he is providing poison to an asp [a deadly snake]."[34]

In contrast, Spartan society encouraged both intellectual and athletic training for its young women. Xenophon, who lived among the Spartans for many years, wrote that Spartan girls ran footraces and competed in trials of strength. And according to Plutarch, these young women also wrestled and threw the discus and javelin, which

Preparing for the Athletic Field

When young Greek boys visited a palaestra, *an athletic facility with an open field, to learn and practice wrestling and other events, they maintained certain cleanliness rituals both before and after the sessions, as explained by Robert Flaceliere in his book about daily life in ancient Greece.*

The essential articles which every boy had to take to the *palaestra* . . . included a sponge for washing himself down, a small oil flask, a bronze scraper . . . [or strigil, which was] a sort of grooved spatula with a curving end. Before his session he would wash at a fountain. . . . He would then rub oil all over his body, and finally sprinkle himself with sand, or dust, letting it run through his fingers in a fine spray. This practice was justified on the grounds that it . . . protect[ed] the body against chills and sudden changes of temperature. When the period of exercise was over, the strigil was essential for scraping off the mixed coat of oil, dust, and sweat that had accumulated on the skin. Afterwards, of course, the boy washed himself all over again.

Athenian women, like these working with yarn, did not receive formal educations.

with vigor and would meet the challenge of childbirth in a successful, relaxed way."[35] In addition, Plato mentions that Spartan girls were trained in music and other arts and that they prided themselves on their intellectual development. This development must have included reading and writing because Sparta produced a number of female poets in the Classical Age; by contrast, Athens produced none.

gave them "a strong start in [building] strong bodies . . . while the women themselves would also bear their pregnancies

Thus, Athens largely wasted most of the vast potential of its young women by excluding them from formal education. Meanwhile, Sparta wasted much of the equally large potential of its young men by training them exclusively for war. Had these unenlightened, unwise attitudes and practices been reversed and replaced with a well-rounded education for all children, Greek society would have been much stronger and more resilient. It would likely have been better able to deal with the forces that eventually overcame it; and if so, history may have been very different.

Slaves: Their Roles in the Home and in Society

Although Athens and many other Greek city-states had democracies or other citizen-run governments in the Classical and Hellenistic periods, not all individuals who lived in these states were citizens and enjoyed the benefits of full civic rights. Usually a person had to be born in a city-state to be a citizen. Foreigners living there (including both non-Greeks and Greeks from other states) did not have citizen status. In Athens, for example, resident foreigners were known as metics (*metoikoi*), who were mostly merchants and artisans. They could not take part in government or own land, but they did make important contributions to the community by paying taxes and providing essential goods and services. Resident foreigners in Sparta were called *perioikoi*, which meant "dwellers round about," reflecting that they were segregated in their own villages on the outskirts of the citizen villages. This was because the *perioikoi*, like Athenian metics, were seen as inferior or subordinate to citizens.

But at least the resident aliens in Athens, Sparta, and elsewhere were free. The many slaves kept in all of the Greek states were unfree and had no legal or civic rights. Slavery was never as widespread in Greece as it eventually became in Rome (which had the largest slavery institution in ancient times), but slaves did a large proportion of the physical labor in all social areas and occupations in Greece. And beginning in the late Archaic Age, slavery was a major factor in Greek home life and the workforces of the community.

How Society Viewed Slavery

As other ancient peoples did, the Greeks accepted the existence of slavery as part of the natural way of things, a condition fully condoned by the gods. Even profound thinkers such as Plato and Aristotle, who proposed ways to improve society and the human condition, could not imagine a society operating efficiently without slave labor. In his *Politics*, Aristotle defined a slave as "a human being who by nature does not belong to himself but to another person." Further, a slave was "a piece of property as well as being human." Aristotle echoed the belief of the majority of people when he said:

> A man who is able to belong to another person is by nature a slave (for that

is why he belongs to someone else). . . . Nature must therefore have intended to make the bodies of free men and of slaves different also; slaves' bodies [are] strong for the services they have to do, those of free men upright and not much use for that kind of work, but instead useful for community [i.e., political] life. [36]

Even the slaves themselves thought slavery was a natural and inevitable situation. This is proven by the fact that many of the slaves who managed to earn their freedom proceeded to acquire slaves of their own.

Another common societal view of slaves was that they were mentally and morally deficient, dishonest, or otherwise bad by nature. So they could not be trusted and

Slaves are sold on an auction block in a Greek city. Like other ancient peoples, the Greeks viewed slavery as a natural institution.

had to be supervised or watched almost constantly. In Xenophon's *Householder,* the country gentleman Ischomachus (who is a thinly veiled version of Xenophon himself) asserts:

> I don't think I have found any cases of good servants with a bad master; I've seen cases of bad servants with a good master, however. But the servants didn't get away with it! . . . [A master or his overseer] must be capable of supervising and scrutinizing the work,

must be prepared to show gratitude for work performed well, and must not be afraid of administering punishment when irresponsibility demands it. [37]

Similarly, most slaves depicted in Greek comic plays were shifty, devious, scheming, lazy, dishonest, cowardly, sex crazed, or some combination of these negative traits. (Yet they were also often portrayed as clever and humorous, traits to be admired.)

Further complicating ancient Greek views of slavery was the widespread belief

A Philosopher Argues That Slavery Is Just

In this excerpt from his Politics *(J.A. Sinclair's translation), Aristotle defines the slave and argues that slavery is natural.*

A human being who by nature does not belong to himself but to another person—such a one is by nature a slave. A human being belongs to another when he is a piece of property as well as being human. A piece of property is a tool which is used to assist some activity, and which has a separate existence of its own. . . . All men who differ from one another by as much as the soul differs from the body or man from a wild beast . . . these people are slaves by nature, and it is better for them to be subject to this kind of control. . . . For a man who is able to belong to another person is by nature a slave (for that is why he belongs to someone else). . . . Nature must therefore have intended to make the bodies of free men and of slaves different also; slaves' bodies [are] strong for the services they have to do, those of free men upright and not much use for that kind of work, but instead useful for community [i.e., political] life. . . . Of course the opposite often happens—slaves can have the bodies of free men, free men only the souls and not the bodies of free men. . . . To conclude: it is clear that there are certain people who are free and certain who are slaves by nature, and it is both to their advantage, and just, for them to be slaves.

that the "natural slave" argument did not necessarily apply to Greeks, who were somehow inherently superior to non-Greeks. In this biased and rather arrogant scenario, a Greek who became a slave to a foreigner had simply fallen into a bad situation and was still free in mind and soul; whereas a non-Greek was a slave by nature, so in becoming a slave he got what he deserved and fulfilled nature's plan. In the words of one Greek writer:

> When an Athenian is taken prisoner in war and shipped off to Persia . . . and sold there, we don't say that such a free man is now a slave. On the other hand, if some . . . Persian is brought here . . . we don't accept that he is free any longer. Now at Athens . . . there is a law which prevents anyone who really is a slave from ever attaining the status of citizen. But no one would deny citizenship to [a Greek] if he had . . . been captured [and made a slave in a foreign land and then returned to Athens]. [38]

Aristotle put it more simply and bluntly when he wrote, "We have to recognize that some people are slaves under any circumstances, and others under none." [39]

Considering these views, it was seen as wrong for Greeks to enslave other Greeks. The most glaring example of the abuse of this unwritten rule was Sparta's conquest of the neighboring state of Messenia in the 600s B.C. and the enslavement of its inhabitants. They became known as helots and were treated extremely harshly. But no other Greeks had the gumption to help them until Sparta's widely feared army was brought to its knees by the forces of Thebes in the Battle of Leuktra in 371 B.C. After that, with the Thebans' help, the Messenians regained their freedom.

Sources, Numbers, and Jobs of Household Slaves

Over the centuries, therefore, most Greek slaves were non-Greeks. Typically they were captured in wars or bought from slave traders, although much smaller numbers were bred in the home. In the Classical Age, they came mostly from Asia Minor or Thrace (the region lying north and northeast of the Aegean Sea); in Hellenistic times and later, when Rome controlled Greece, some Greek slaves came from more distant regions, including the coasts of the Black Sea and the isle of Britain.

The exact numbers of slaves who lived and worked in Greek homes and shops are uncertain. But the consensus of modern scholars is that a household of moderate means probably had two or three slaves and a well-to-do family perhaps fifteen to twenty. Of these household slaves, it is likely that a higher proportion were women than men. Perhaps this is partly because household jobs were generally viewed as "women's work." The female domestic slaves helped with the spinning, weaving, sewing, cooking, and cleaning, and nursed babies and watched over the family children. Sometimes a slave woman managed an entire household for her owners. Probably this occurred most often in cases where a well-to-do man owned

A slave spins yarn in this drawing. Greek slaves performed menial tasks, ran errands, and looked after children.

a country home that needed to be kept up when he and his family were living in town. Xenophon's Ischomachus, who owned such an estate, recalled choosing a housekeeper:

> We had appointed . . . the woman whom we considered . . . to be the most self-disciplined with regard to food, drink, sleep, and sex, and who, in addition, struck us as having the best memory and being most likely to avoid incurring our disfavor by neglecting her duties. . . . We taught her to be prepared to work hard for the increase of our estate. . . . We also

instilled justice [honesty] in her, by rewarding right, not wrong, among the servants and by showing her that justice leads to a wealthier and freer life than injustice. [40]

In many Greek households, female slaves were also expected to perform sexual favors for the master. In Xenophon's *Householder,* Ischomachus declares that when his young wife is wearing makeup and dressed nicely "she becomes an object of desire, and especially because she is granting her favors willingly." In contrast, he says, "the servant has no choice but to submit." [41] And a character in a dialogue by a later ancient writer asks, "Don't many Athenians have sex with their slave women, some of them secretly and some even openly?" [42] Care must be taken not to judge such practices so common in ancient times by modern standards. Today, sexual exploitation of this kind is recognized as rape, or at least as serious abuse; but in the Greco-Roman world, it was widely accepted, like slavery itself, as natural and inevitable.

Though generally outnumbered by their female counterparts, male household slaves had numerous important tasks. They performed repairs, both inside and outside, did the shopping (or helped the master do it), accompanied the master's son to school, and chaperoned the women of the house when they appeared in public. Male slaves also ran errands, carried messages, and accompanied the master on trips. In rare cases, usually only in a national emergency, some male slaves actually fought alongside their masters in battle.

Commercial, Agricultural, and Public Slave Workers

Both female and male household slaves were significantly outnumbered by those who labored in shops and other commercial enterprises. Evidence shows, for instance, that Lysias and his brother had more than a hundred slaves in their shield-making shop. They had evidently inherited them from their father, a metic named Cephalus, who had established the business.

Slaves also worked in farming jobs, such as planting, pruning, harvesting, threshing, tending animals, and so on. Often, these slaves worked side by side with their owners and/or members of the owner's family. This reflected the common view that it was

all right for free persons to perform such work as long as they were working for themselves. If, by contrast, they did such menial jobs for someone else, they were no better than slaves.

In any case, in the Athenian territory of Attica, as well as in Boeotia and most other parts of Greece, slaves played only a supporting role in agriculture. This is because the societies of Athens and most of its neighbors were dominated by free peasant farmers who worked their own lands, usually with only minimal help. A major exception was Sparta in late Archaic and early Classical times. In those years, the Spartans forced the enslaved helots to take over all aspects of agriculture, thereby completely freeing Spartan citizens to

A farm slave harvests grain. Most small farmers in Greece had few slaves, while wealthy men with large estates could not get by without several.

take part in political, military, and other endeavors. Aristotle actually thought such an exploitive system was ideal and in his *Politics* advocated its adoption by Athens and other city-states:

> The people who cultivate the land should be slaves. They should not all come from the same tribe or nation, and they should not be too courageous. This will make them useful workers and safe from the danger of revolt. As a second best [approach], they should be non-Greek-speaking serfs with natural characters as similar as possible to those I have indicated. Those of them who are used on private estates must be private property, and those used on community land public property. [43]

Aristotle's mention of public slaves is important. The governments of Athens and presumably all or most other Greek states owned slaves to take care of a host of communal menial tasks. In another of his works, the *Athenian Constitution*, Aristotle describes the jobs of slaves who

More Public Slaves Will Increase Prosperity

In his short treatise titled Ways and Means *(in* Scripta Minora*), Xenophon advocates increasing the number of public slaves working in Athens's silver mines. This, he claims, will eventually improve the city's productivity.*

Were my proposals adopted . . . the state would become possessed of public slaves until there were three for every citizen. . . . Assume that the total number of slaves to begin with is twelve hundred. By using the revenue derived from these, the number might in all possibility be raised to six thousand, at least in the course of five or six years. . . . The annual revenue derived from that number of men is sixty *talents*. Out of this sum, if twenty *talents* are invested in additional slaves, the state will have forty *talents* available for any other necessary purpose. And when a total of ten thousand men is reached, the revenue will be a hundred *talents*. . . . The [revenues] derived from the slaves would not be the only source of relief to the community. With the concentration of a large population in the mining district, abundant revenue would be derived from the local market [and] from state-owned houses near the silver mines. . . . If the plans I have put forward are carried out . . . we shall become a people . . . better disciplined and more efficient in war.

aided Athens's elected officials and administrators:

> They keep watch to prevent any scavengers from depositing [manure and other refuse] within a mile and a quarter of the [town] wall. And they prevent the construction of buildings encroaching on and balconies overhanging the roads; and they remove for burial the bodies of persons who die on the roads.[44]

Later in the same document, Aristotle says that another job of public slaves is to repair the roads. (In Greece in Classical times, most roads were unpaved; so repairs consisted of clearing fallen trees and other refuse, filling potholes, and, where gravel surfaces existed, adding and spreading new gravel.) Another public slave job materialized in about 100 B.C., when Athenian leaders turned over the task of overseeing weights and measures in Attica's marketplaces to slaves. A surviving inscription describes the work involved and advocates corporal punishment for those slaves who try to take advantage of their positions:

> They must provide equivalents of the weights and measures to the government officials and to all other persons who ask for them . . . and they must not carry anything out of the buildings provided, except for the lead or copper equivalents. But if they [attempt to carry away silver] . . . [the officials] are to punish the slave[s] . . . by whipping.[45]

Some Slaves Were Treated Badly

Another class of public slaves in Athens consisted of the workers who toiled in the state-owned silver mines at Laureum in southern Attica. It was with the riches derived from these operations that the city built the fleet that defeated the Persians in 480 B.C. and helped Athens rise to greatness in the years that followed. Without these slaves and their labors, therefore, free Athenians would not have created one of the world's most splendid golden ages. Yet these slaves to whom Athens owed so much were treated with despicable cruelty. They were shackled day and night, forced to work in horrendous conditions, and had no hope of gaining their freedom.

The Spartan helots were not much better off. They greatly outnumbered native Spartan citizens, who worried constantly that the slaves might rebel. (In fact, they did rebel in 464 B.C., following an earthquake that rocked Sparta, and it took five years for the Spartans to regain the upper hand.) Fear of rebellion was part of the rationale for the harsh and at times inhuman treatment the helots endured. In addition to backbreaking work from sunup to sundown and beatings for the slightest infraction, they were subject to state-supported murder committed by young men in military training. According to Plutarch:

> Periodically, the overseers of the young men would dispatch them into the countryside . . . equipped with daggers and basic rations, but nothing

Slaves work alongside free laborers on a temple. Athens and other prosperous Greek cities used slaves for public building projects.

else. . . . At night, they made their way to roads and murdered any helot whom they caught. Frequently, too, they made their way through the fields, killing the helots who stood out for their physique and strength. [46]

Plutarch also describes Spartan humiliation of helots:

They would force them, for instance, to drink quantities of unmixed wine [the Greeks normally drank their wine diluted with water] and then would bring them into the mess halls to show the young men what drunkenness was like. They would also order them to perform songs and dances which were vulgar and ludicrous. [47]

Another form of ill treatment endured by slaves all over Greece was the practice of torturing them to secure evidence in court cases. The rationale was that, being inferior and dishonest by nature, a slave was not likely to tell the truth except under duress. At least a few owners objected to this, believing it to be unnecessary and cruel. In a court speech written by Lysias, the defendant is indignant that the man accusing him of wrongdoing refuses to allow his slave woman, an eyewitness, to be tortured:

If *I* had refused to submit my [own] slaves to torture, it would have counted against the credibility of my statements. I ask that it will count equally as testimony to my truthfulness that the prosecutor refused to get proof out of the woman. . . . As things are, I am in danger of exile from my country, and yet I am not going to be allowed even to get the truth out of her regarding the charges on which I am standing my trial. It would have been far more just that she be tortured. [48]

Most Slaves Were Treated Well

In contrast, most Greek slaves were never called to testify at court, lived outside of Sparta, and did not work in mines. The majority were household or shop slaves or assistants to town officials, all of whom were generally well treated. Household slaves in particular often became trusted members of the family. Part of this good treatment stemmed from feelings of human decency and kindness. Yet there is little doubt that a good many masters took excellent care of their slaves first and foremost because they were valuable property that could not be fully exploited when physically injured or emotionally upset.

Thus, although some owners likely struck or flogged their household slaves from time to time, both custom and law usually prevented severe brutality. In Athens, a free person who beat or killed another person's

Getting Slaves to Obey

In his Oeconomicus *(or* Householder*), Xenophon offers the following advice (quoted from Tredennick's and Waterfield's translation in* Conversations of Socrates *) on how to make slaves more obedient without resorting to physical coercion.*

There are two ways in which the rest of the animal kingdom learns obedience—by being punished when they attempt to be disobedient, and by being rewarded when they willingly do what they're supposed to do. . . . Human beings can be made more obedient just by force of argument, by proving it is in their interest to obey. But where slaves are concerned, the training which is apparently designed only for lower animals is very effective for teaching obedience. For you'll get plenty of results by gratifying their bellies in accordance with their desires. Those of them with ambitious temperaments can also be motivated by praise. . . . By using this training method, the [slaves] I deal with become more obedient.

slave could be prosecuted. In addition, it was illegal for an owner to kill his own slave, no matter what crime the slave committed, as shown in a speech, directed to a jury, written by the Athenian orator Antiphon in about 419 B.C.:

> Even slaves who kill their masters, even if they are caught red-handed are not [allowed to be] put to death by the relatives of the deceased. The . . . relatives hand them over to the authorities, in accordance with [Athens's] laws. The law allows . . . a slave to give evidence against a free man in a . . . murder charge, and allows a master, if he so . . . desires, to prosecute anyone who kills his slave. The law has equal force against a man who kills a . . . slave and against him who kills a free man. [49]

Ironically, part of the evidence that many Greek slaves were well treated comes from the testimony of an old-fashioned man who felt they were *too* well treated! An anonymous late fifth-century B.C. writer, whom modern scholars have come to call the "Old Oligarch" asserted:

> Among the slaves and metics at Athens there is the greatest uncontrolled wantonness. You can't hit them there, and a slave will not stand aside for you [when you meet him in the street]. . . . If it were customary for a slave . . . to be struck by one who is free, you would often hit an Athenian citizen by mistake on the assumption that he was

a slave. For the people there are no better dressed than slaves and metics. [50]

Manumission and the Work of Freedmen

Another indication of the generally decent treatment of Greek household slaves is the fact that they sometimes received small wages, probably better described as periodic tips for good behavior. A slave could spend this money. Or he or she could save up to buy his or her freedom, which a kind master might also grant as a reward for long years of trusted service.

The freeing of a slave, called manumission, was often accomplished through a written contract. (Apparently a master could free a slave simply by verbal declaration; however, this could be hard to prove if disputed later, especially if the former owner was now mentally incapacitated or dead.) Several of these agreements have survived, carved onto the walls of public buildings. One reads, in part, "On the following conditions, Sophrona [the owner], acting with the consent of her son Sosandros, hands over . . . to be free the female house-born slave named Onasiphoron." [51]

One drawback to manumission in ancient Greece was that the freed slave, or freedman, was usually obligated to spend a certain number of years in the former owner's employ. Sometimes the period stipulated was the remainder of the master's life. As another clause from Onasiphoron's contract shows, in such a case the freedman was not all that better off than before:

Onasiphoron is to remain with Sophrona for the whole period of the latter's life, doing whatever she is ordered to do without giving cause or complaint. If she does not do so, then Sophrona is to have the power to punish her in whatever way she wishes. And Onasiphoron is to give Sosandros a child [i.e., to have his baby]. [52]

Once free, former Athenian slaves had the same social status as metics, which meant that they had no political rights and could not own land. So usually, such freedmen had no other choice but to continue working in the jobs they were in when they were slaves. In a freedman's favor, however, was the fact that now he could be more than a mere laborer with no say in how the business operated; instead, the freedman could become a part or full owner of the business and share in its profits. Moreover, like a metic, the freedman could become as financially successful as circumstances allowed. And evidently on occasion some former slaves became very successful indeed. When he died in 370 B.C., a freedman named Paison was the richest manufacturer in Athens and left his heirs an extremely valuable estate.

Such success stories were extremely rare, as the vast majority of Greek slaves never tasted freedom. And the situation did not improve in Greece's Hellenistic and Roman periods. Despite the occasional protestations by Greek and Roman philosophers and early Christian thinkers that slaves were as inherently worthy as free people, no one, including the Christians, seriously proposed eradicating slavery. As a result, menial work in the Greco-Roman world, both at home and in the community, remained mainly the province and burden of people with no social status, no political voice, and no choice but to obey.

Home Life: Food, Clothes, and Private Worship

Whether they were free or slave, rich or poor, all Greeks had in common certain basic domestic customs and habits. These included the foods they ate and how they were prepared and preserved, the kinds and styles of clothes they wore, their grooming habits, and their personal spiritual beliefs and home-based worship. These aspects of daily life were often interwoven so completely that no one for a moment contemplated one without the other. For example, the vast majority of Greeks were extremely conscious of how they looked and took pains to make sure they were clean, well groomed, and well dressed whenever possible.

Even more striking was the way food and religious worship invariably accompanied, as well as complemented, each other. Most of

the things the Greeks sacrificed to the gods—whether liquid, vegetable, or animal—were edible. People offered the gods a small portion of the food and then consumed the rest themselves. So, on the one hand nothing was wasted, and on the other eating and having a good time was an integral part of the ritual. In the words of Andrew Dalby, an authority on Greek eating habits, "Greek sacrifice, not unlike feast days in many other religious systems, was at the same time a religious observance, an occasion for enjoyment, and an opportunity for meat-eating [then a periodic treat for most people]."[53]

The Ritual of Sacrifice

In addition to honoring the gods in public celebrations involving feasts and sacrifices on specified days of religious observance, Greeks offered a portion of food to the gods at every meal. Yet eating was not the only activity of Greek home life in which religion played a key role. Indeed, belief in and worship of divine beings constituted one of the most essential aspects of Greek life; and some kind of religious ritual accompanied nearly every gathering, function, or important endeavor, both private and public.

In the private sphere, centered on the home and family, religious rituals attended all important life-cycle events. The *amphidromia,* the ceremony that welcomed newborn babies into the family, for example, was accompanied by solemn sacrifices and probably prayers for the well-being of the child. In Athens (and likely in many other Greek states) another ceremony in which people performed sacrifices to honor and appease

the gods was the *apatouria;* this three-day festival, held in October, welcomed new members into the local phratries. (A phratry was an extended kinship group composed of several clans, each clan having a few families.) Religious sacrifices and prayers were also integral and expected parts of wedding ceremonies, family and clan meetings, business deals and other personal ventures, and funeral rituals.

Of these two main aspects of religious observance—sacrifice and prayer—sacrifice was the more formal, elaborate, and important. Although technically one could perform a sacrifice anywhere, in the home this activity usually took place at the family altar, an essential feature of all houses, rich and poor. The altar was situated most often in the central courtyard or the main hearth room. It consisted of a rectangular, often pillarlike stone standing roughly waist high.

This drawing, based on the sculptures that once adorned the Parthenon frieze, shows young men leading bulls toward a public sacrifice.

In poorer homes, the stone hearth itself might double as the family altar. Wealthier households could afford separate altars having elaborate carved decorations like the communal versions that stood beside the public temples.

The set rituals of sacrifice followed traditions handed down from extremely ancient (probably Stone Age) times. One of the most common forms was the libation—the offering of a liquid to the god being honored. Most often it was wine (mixed with water), although milk, olive oil, and honey were also commonly used. It was the custom to place the liquid in a special bowl, usually made of metal, called a *phiale*, and then pour it over the altar. When all of the liquid was offered this way, the libation was called a *khoe*. In contrast, when the worshipper poured a small portion of the wine from his or her drinking cup onto the altar and then drank the rest, the libation was called a *sponde*.

The sacrifice of animals (*thysia*, meaning "burnt offering") was considerably more involved than libations. In preparation, the

A Young Cow Is Sacrificed

In this scene from his Odyssey *(E.V. Rieu's translation), Homer describes the sacrifice of a heifer (young cow) to the goddess Athena. Homer probably lived during the late eighth century* B.C., *which means that these sacrificial rituals originated earlier.*

The heifer was brought in from the meadows. . . . Stratius and Echephron led the heifer forward by the horns, and Aretus came out from the storeroom, carrying in his right hand a flowered bowl of water [for purification] . . . and in the other a basket with the barley-corns [also used to purify], while the stalwart Thrasymedes, gripping a sharp axe, stood by to cut the victim down. . . . Nester now started the ritual with the water and the scattered grain, and offered up his earnest prayers to Athena as he began the sacrifice by throwing a lock from the victim's head on the fire. . . . [Then] Thrasymedes stepped boldly up and struck. The axe cut through the tendons of the heifer's neck and she collapsed. . . . When the dark blood had gushed out, and life had left the heifer's bones, they swiftly dismembered the carcass. . . . [After parts of the beast were burned for the goddess, Nester] sprinkled red wine over the flames, and the young men gathered round with five-pronged forks in their hands. When the thighs were burned up and they had tasted the inner parts, they carved the rest into small pieces, pierced them with skewers and held the sharp ends of the spits to the fire till all was roasted.

person (or persons) performing the ritual washed his or her hands to purify them (in a symbolic way, not for hygienic purposes) and used water to purify the altar as well. Then the worshippers placed garlands of flowers over the animal, which they referred to as the victim. Because of the confined space of the average house, the animals sacrificed at home were likely usually small. Common ones included goats, lambs, hares, dogs, fish, and birds.

When everything was ready, the worshippers led the victim to the altar. There, one of them (usually the male head of the household) sprinkled barley grains on the victim to purify it further. Then the person used a sharp knife to cut the animal's throat, drained the blood into a bowl, and sprinkled some of it on the altar, and/or over the other worshippers. Next, it was time to slaughter the victim with knives and axes. The people wrapped the bones and organs in the animal's fat and burned the offering on the altar, generating smoke that they believed would float up and both nourish and appease the god. Finally, the worshippers divided, cooked, and ate the meat from the animal. In the *Odyssey*, Homer describes the beginning of the ceremonial feast after the sacrifice of a small cow:

> The young men gathered round with five-pronged forks in their hands. When the thighs were burned up and they had tasted the inner parts, they carved the rest into small pieces, pierced them with skewers and held

the sharp ends of the spits to the fire till all was roasted. [54]

Other Religious Rituals and Beliefs

The other main aspect of Greek religious worship—prayer—often accompanied births, marriages, travel departures, funerals, and so on. There were certain formulas one followed for each—set words and phrases, in the same vein as the "Hail Marys" recited by modern Catholics. But as is also common today, the Greeks uttered individualized, personal, private prayers. Usually one asked a god to grant blessings of some kind, which might be in the form of material gains, such as money or fame. Or the blessing might be nonmaterial as well as more humble, as in the case of a surviving prayer attributed to the philosopher Socrates: "Beloved Pan [an important woodland god] . . . give me beauty in the inward soul. And may the outward and inward man be at one. May I reckon the wise to be the wealthy." [55]

Whatever the nature of the prayer, a Greek almost always delivered it while standing, with his or her hands raised, palms upward. The Greeks viewed kneeling in prayer, which is the most common position taken today, as unworthy of a free person. If the god being addressed dwelled below ground, the worshipper might stretch his or her arms downward or stomp on the ground to get the god's attention. Also, prayers were usually said aloud unless the worshipper had some special reason to conceal them.

A young boar is about to be sacrificed in this painting on an ancient drinking cup.

Other spiritual practices and beliefs that affected the Greeks in their everyday life come under the general heading of divination. In one way or another, these involved prophecy, omens (special signs of impending good or bad fortune), and other means of divining future events. For example, most people believed that omens could be detected by examining animals' livers or other organs, birds' behavior and flight formations, or patterns of thunder and lightning. Astrology (connecting human behavior to the movements of the heavenly bodies) was seen as another way to foretell the future.

Likewise, various happenings and visions in dreams might foreshadow events to come. Because dreams came during sleep, which was a home-based activity, the interpretation of dreams and any changed routines based on those interpretations were an integral part of home life. Like many other ancient peoples, the Greeks accepted that the contents of dreams had specific meanings and that the gods sometimes used dreams either to reveal the future or offer people guidance. The famous Greek physician Galen, for example, supposedly took up medicine because of something his father observed in a dream. Also, Asclepius, the god of healing, was thought to visit sick people in dreams and provide them with advice about cures (a practice known as incubation). Greeks everywhere attached much meaning to the following lines from a play by the fifth-century B.C. Athenian playwright Euripides:

Strange shapes stirred in the womb of the ground [when Apollo, the god of prophecy, took charge of the holy grounds at Delphi, a shrine in central Greece], and visiting dreams of night were born, and flew to the sleeping cities of men when darkness and deep rest had laid them still, and told them of things past and things to come.[56]

Some people tried to interpret dreams, omens, and other divine signs themselves. But many turned to someone with a reputation for expertise in such matters. In some cases, a person in the immediate or extended family (possibly in one's clan or phratry) had this special talent. It was also common to consult professional soothsayers, usually itinerant (traveling) characters. For a price, they would come to someone's house and explain the meanings of omens, dreams, and other mysteries. The problem was that, as remains true today, most people who offered such services were con artists who preyed on the gullible. Plato described with disdain soothsayers who knocked on "rich men's doors" and offered all sorts of "magic arts and incantations" that would supposedly get the forces of nature "to do their will."[57]

Common Foods

It is important to note that, although worship of some kind took place in a Greek home on a daily basis, animal sacrifice and the consumption of the meat accompanying it did not. Such sacrifices, both at home and in the communal worship that took place at public temples, occurred mainly during periodic religious festivals. The rest

The Greek View of the Divine

The Greeks were polytheistic, which means that they worshipped multiple deities. The major gods were known as the Olympians because early traditions claimed they dwelled atop Mt. Olympus, the tallest mountain in Greece. (By the Classical Age, this had become a fable and those who believed in the gods held that they lived in a distant part of the sky or in an invisible realm.) Among the leading gods were Zeus, who ruled the others; his wife, Hera, protector of marriage and children; Poseidon, Zeus's brother and ruler of the seas; Artemis, goddess of wild animals and protector of young girls; Apollo, god of truth and prophecy; Ares, the war god; and Athena, goddess of wisdom and war (and Athens's patron deity). The Greeks saw these gods as having human form and emotions. Zeus and the others made mistakes, fought among themselves, and had marriages, love affairs, and children. Consequently, the Greeks did not perceive the gods as holy or morally perfect, as is common in many modern faiths. Instead, the average Greek deeply respected the gods for their physical beauty and especially their great power, which was the main factor that separated these divinities from humans. The general belief was that this power could either provide for human civilization or utterly destroy it. "Single the race, single of men and gods," sang the fifth-century B.C. Greek poet Pindar (C.M. Bowra's translation). "From a single mother we both draw breath. But a difference of power in everything keeps us apart."

of the time, most Greeks did not eat beef and only occasionally consumed pork, lamb, fowl, and deer at their main meals. (Exceptions were a few wealthy people who ate these meats more often.)

Much more common for both rich and poor Greeks, however, was the consumption of fish. Because a majority of the larger Greek cities and towns were located on seashores, fish was easily available to most people at a reasonable price. And for the fishermen themselves and their immediate neighbors in the port cities, it was a staple food (as opposed to the countryside, where

A vase from fifth-century B.C. Athens shows a merchant selling fish.

fish was less available and not a staple). Indeed, as Dalby points out, gastronomy (the art of good cooking and eating) in Greek city homes was intimately connected to the preparation and eating of fish and other kinds of seafood:

Nothing is more striking than the difference between the commonplaces of gastronomic literature in Greece and Rome. While Roman poets were to boast of their farms and their fresh produce, Greeks wrote of the fish they bought at market and the prices they paid. . . . The fourth-century B.C. gourmet [food expert and lover] Archestratus helps to make this clear. Forty-eight of the surviving passages from [his writings] are about fish, and only eleven are on other topics. . . . In his time . . . fish rather than meat was evidently the luxury food that was available for purchase. . . . Gastronomy grew in Greek cities as the fresh fish market grew. They went together, and they cannot be separated from the spread of urban households with an income derived from business rather than land. It is no coincidence if Sparta lacked all three—a business population, a market for fish, [and] an enthusiasm for the "life of pleasure." [58]

Still, although fish was the most common kind of animal flesh eaten in ancient Greece, it was not the mainstay of the average diet. Instead, most people lived primarily on grains, fruits, and vegetables, usually consumed in moderate quantities. (Indeed, individual portions of all foods were considerably smaller than those eaten today; and as a result, obesity, which is a serious problem in the United States, was almost unheard-of in ancient Greece.) The grains included barley and wheat. Of these, wheat was the more expensive and unreliable because it did not grow well in most parts of Greece. So, large city-states like Athens imported most of their wheat from foreign ports, especially those on the shores of the Black Sea. Common fruits included figs, pears, apples, pomegranates, plums, sour cherries, watermelons, grapes, and olives. Staple vegetables included, among many others, beets, lentils, cabbage, lettuce, basil, garlic, onions, mushrooms, mustard greens, radishes, and cucumbers. Almonds, walnuts, hazelnuts, and other nuts were also popular. And cheese (made mainly from goat's milk) and eggs were eaten liberally, while the main sweetener in Greek cooking and baking was honey.

As there was no refrigeration in ancient times, preserving these foodstuffs was, depending on the item, either impossible or laborious. Meat and fish were dried, salted, or smoked to make them last longer. Some fruits, notably grapes, figs, and plums, were preserved by drying (which turned grapes into raisins, of course), and people pickled a number of fruits and vegetables as well as some varieties of fish. Considering the lack of knowledge of germs and proper sanitary practices at the time, contamination and food poisoning were almost certainly more common than they are today.

This ancient olive oil press features a heavy stone roller.

Wine, Olive Oil, and Mealtimes

The most common beverage by far in ancient Greece was wine. Its importance, along with that of olive oil, in the Greek diet cannot be overstressed. Wild forms of grapes and olives existed when humans first settled Greece, tens of thousands of years ago, and people gathered and ate them. But when they began cultivating them in a careful, systematic fashion, they produced both more and better versions. Thereafter, grapes and olives became essential staples of the Greek diet, although usually neither was consumed in its original form during the main course of a meal. Dalby explains:

> Both provided cooking media and flavorings, the olive with its oil, the grape with its juice, both unfermented and

Many ancient Greek pitchers for pouring wine have survived. The five depicted here are as beautiful as they are functional.

fermented into wine. It is a challenging hint of conservatism at the center of the menu that grape, wine, and olive were not visibly present in the main course of a classical Greek meal. Whatever the use of olive oil in cooking, and as a medium for sauces, olives themselves were eaten only before the meal as an appetizer. Whatever the use of . . . wine in cooking, wine was served to diners only after they had eaten.[59]

The wine was almost always diluted with water in a ratio of roughly two parts water to one part wine. A special bowl-like container, called a crater (*krater*), evolved specif-

ically for mixing wine. Most Greeks liked their wine chilled. Storing it underground was the most common method in warm weather, although for special occasions those who could afford it had slaves haul in ice from the nearest mountains.

As Dalby points out, olive oil was the number-one cooking medium in ancient Greece and the foundation of numerous sauces. The oil was also used as fuel for oil lamps to light house interiors at night, to make skin oils and perfumes, and for oiling the body to keep it clean. To extract the oil from the olives, people first crushed them. For many centuries this was done by grinding them in a bowl using a mortar and pestle; eventually (perhaps by Hellenistic times),

A Recipe for Meat Stew

In his fascinating book Siren Feasts, *about ancient Greek foods and cooking, scholar Andrew Dalby includes this surviving ancient recipe for cooking goat, lamb, or chicken.*

When you prepare fresh-killed kid or lamb or even chicken as food, put some fresh wheat grains, crushed, in a deep pan, and stir [them] up together with fragrant [olive] oil. [Cook the meat in a separate pot and] when the stew is boiling, pour it over [the crushed wheat] and cover it with the lid, for when so treated, the heavy meal swells up [with the oil and meat juices]. Serve, just warm, with bread.

Servants cut up the remains of a sheep in preparation for a feast in this painting on an ancient mixing bowl.

the Greeks began using a large stone saucer in which two millstones revolved and crushed the olives. After that, they pressed the olives to squeeze out the oil, as described by scholars Lesley and Roy A. Adkins:

> This could be done by various means, such as placing a heavy weight on bags or baskets of olives. A simple mechanical press was also used, consisting of a large wooden beam that was anchored at one end and acted as a lever. Crushed olives were placed in a permeable [porous] container (possibly of cloth) on a hard surface beneath the lever, and the other end of the lever was forced downward to squash the container and its contents. . . . The pressing was usually done on a wooden or stone pressing bed, with a channel and spout to collect the oil.[60]

The regular meals in which olive oil, wine, and other foodstuffs were consumed varied in number and size over the centuries. It is not surprising that eating habits changed, particularly considering that ancient Greek civilization lasted for nearly two thousand years and, like all cultures do, tended to evolve and fluctuate over time. In much of the Archaic Age and probably well before, most Greeks appear to have eaten a light breakfast soon after sunrise. This was followed by a large afternoon meal, the biggest of the day, and a lighter supper after dark.

By contrast, in the Classical Age people tended to skip breakfast. Instead, they ate a light lunch, called *ariston,* and the main meal, *deipnon,* in the evening. The chief fare at lunch consisted of bread, cheese, and fruit; and at supper, bread, vegetables, porridge (made from barley or wheat), lentil soup, sometimes fish, and occasionally meat, followed by cake, nuts, and/or fruit for dessert. Toward the end of Classical times, however, breakfast (*akratisma*) became more common again and remained so for several centuries to come. As in the past, it was a light meal, consisting of a little bread (sometimes soaked in wine) and perhaps a bit of cheese or fruit. Family members, both male and female, usually ate together, except when the head of the household entertained his guests in the *andron,* in which case the women and small children dined separately.

Common Clothing Styles and Accessories

If the Greeks' staple foods were fairly basic (with only a few wealthy people seeking more exotic fare) and their eating habits moderate, the same can be said for their clothes. Most urban Greeks placed a premium on cleanliness and dressing neatly. Their typical outfits (which influenced fashions across the ancient Mediterranean world) were simple in shape and design but were very comfortable and attractive. For the most part, the nature of these designs was dictated and limited by the shape of the looms that produced the cloth for clothes. Looms were rectangular. So they produced rectangular pieces of cloth that people then draped and fastened around their bodies in a number of ways. Thus, very little cloth was

Left to right: a chiton (tunic); an exomis *(tunic with part placed around the left shoulder); a chiton with a himation; and a himation worn alone.*

wasted and the need for time-consuming hand sewing was minimal.

The most common garment for both men and women was the basic tunic, or chiton. Consisting of a rectangular piece of cloth stitched up the sides, it had holes cut for the head and arms and hung skirtlike at the bottom. Men generally wore the tunic knee length, although ankle length was the rule for elderly men and for men of all ages on formal occasions. Young women sometimes wore their tunics knee length, especially in Sparta; but custom dictated ankle length for most Greek women, who often used buttons, pins, or brooches rather than stitching to secure the garment's sides and top.

Another basic and universal item of attire, also worn by both genders, was the himation. Essentially it was a very large rectangular piece of cloth that people wrapped around

the body in various ways, usually over the tunic. A himation could act as a protective cloak to keep a person warm and dry, as traveling attire, or as part of formal wear, depending on the situation. Robert Flaceliere explains how a person put on a himation:

> First the wearer spread it over his shoulders and back, letting the two lower corners hang down in front of him. Then, with his outstretched right arm, he grasped the free folds and passed them either over his left arm (which was bent to accommodate them) or else over his left shoulder, whence they hung down behind. [61]

Because one grasped the himation in the right hand and threw it over the left side of the body, the Greeks called this process "dressing to the right." Generally, those who did not follow this custom were seen as country bumpkins or social misfits. In one of his dialogues, Plato has the eccentric philosopher Socrates complain about a fellow who does not know "how to wear his cloak like a gentleman."[62]

Otherwise, there was considerable flexibility in the way one draped a himation. A now famous statue of the playwright Sophocles has both of his arms enveloped by the garment, with only the right hand protruding from beneath. Other approaches were to tuck the lateral fold of the himation under the chin or to wrap it over the head like a hood. These methods had the drawback of confining the arms. So public orators like Demosthenes and his frequent political opponent Aeschines tucked the cloak under, rather than over, their right arms, then carried it over the chest and left shoulder. This left their right arms free to gesture and add emphasis and drama to their speeches.

The Greeks added many accessories to these basic garments. Young men and soldiers often wore an outer cloak called a *chlamys,* which they fastened at one shoulder with a brooch or pin. And in formal situations, women wore colorful scarves and shawls over their himations. As for footwear, some Greeks, especially in the countryside, went barefoot in warm weather. But it is was probably more common, especially in the cities, to wear leather sandals; and leather shoes and boots were often worn in the colder months. Because of the hot Mediterranean sun, hats were frequently donned for protection. Particularly common was the *petasos,* which had a wide brim and a cord on which the hat hung

The two drawings on the left show a woman donning an ankle-length chiton; at right, a chiton worn plain and one overlaid by a shawl.

A drawing based on surviving Greek toilet items, including a hand mirror, body scraper, fans, and containers for bath oils and perfumes.

when the person temporarily flipped it off the head.

Greek Grooming

Good grooming went hand in hand with neat dressing in Greece's Classical Age. This was true of most men, who kept their beards well trimmed. (Almost all men wore beards until early Hellenistic times, when the clean-shaven look became widely popular.) It was even more true of women, for whom grooming, makeup, and hairstyles were as important as they are for modern women. According to noted scholar Sarah B. Pomeroy, Greek women removed their pubic hair by singeing [scorching with a flame] and plucking. Cosmetics were used by housewives as well as by prostitutes. A white complexion was considered attractive, since it proved that a woman was wealthy enough not to go out in the sun. Powder of white lead was commonly used for this, and . . . rouge was used on the cheeks. Although dress was simple, jewelry and hairdos could be complicated. Women wore their hair loose, surmounted by a coronet or headband, or up in a chignon [knot] or net. False curls seem to have been used sometimes. Slaves' hair, however, was usually cropped. [63]

It is uncertain how many Greek men preferred their wives to wear makeup and how many did not. We do know that Xenophon fell into the second group. In a charming scene in the *Householder*, the conservative Ischomachus lectures his wife that the natural look is better: "The gods have made horses attract horses, cows cows, and sheep sheep. Human beings are no different. They find an unadorned human body the most attractive." [64] Even today, practically everyone knows someone who agrees with Xenophon on this point; this is a reminder that, though religious beliefs and dress styles tend to change over time, human nature does not.

Work: Common Male and Female Occupations

As in so many other areas of ancient Greek life, attitudes toward work and various occupations changed considerably over time. The economies of the Greek states were based mainly on agriculture, and independent small landowners were society's predominant workers for many centuries. In the Archaic Age, a farmer, through his labors, fed his family; and throughout the countryside most homes were otherwise nearly self-sufficient, as the women and slaves made the clothes, and so on. One result was that farming came to be seen as the preferable, and even as the only really honorable, profession for free citizens, especially those from well-to-do families. Craftsmen, artisans, and merchants, who sold the fruits of their labors to the masses,

and especially people who worked directly for someone else in exchange for money, were seen as less reputable. Xenophon later summed it up this way:

> The manual crafts, as they are called, have a bad name and are not rated at all highly in our countries [i.e., city-states]. There are good reasons for this. You see, those who work at them . . . are forced to be sedentary and spend their time out of sunlight. . . . As a result, their bodies are ruined, and this . . . is accompanied by considerable weakening of their minds, too. These so-called manual crafts give people no time to bother with friends or [defending the] country. . . . In fact, it is a rule

Creating Work for the Masses

Here, from his Life of Pericles *(Ian Scott-Kilvert's translation), Plutarch tells how Pericles created work for many of his countrymen by initiating massive building projects (including the erection of the Parthenon) that required the services of hundreds, and at times thousands, of people.*

[Pericles said:] "Once completed, [these public works] will bring [Athens] glory for all time, and while they are being built will convert that surplus to immediate use. In this way all kinds of enterprises and demands will be created which will provide inspiration for every art, find employment for every hand, and transform the whole people into wage-earners, so that the city will decorate and maintain herself at the same time from her own resources." He was also anxious that the unskilled masses, who had no military training, should not be debarred from benefiting from the national income, and yet should not be paid for sitting about and doing nothing. So he boldly laid before the people proposals for immense public works and plans for buildings, which would involve many different arts and industries and require long periods to complete.

in some countries, and especially those with a reputation for military prowess [a specific reference to Sparta], that only non-citizens can work at manual crafts.[65]

Though Xenophon wrote this in the second half of the Classical Age, his attitude was not reflective of society as a whole in his day. In the first half of that crucial era, Athens and other large Greek states expanded in size and became highly urbanized. Farming remained important; but many thousands of people now lived in urban townhouses, bought their food in the town marketplace, and purchased some of their clothes and many luxury items from local shops. As a result, trade and local industries expanded.

Also, huge construction projects were initiated across Greece in this age, the most famous being the great temple complex atop Athens's Acropolis. These required the services of many skilled artisans and other workers. The wide range of jobs created is well illustrated by Plutarch's well-known description of the materials and workers who erected the Acropolis complex:

The materials to be used were stone, bronze, ivory, gold, ebony, and cypress-wood, while the arts or trades which wrought or fashioned them were those of carpenter, modeler, coppersmith, stone-mason, dyer, worker in gold and ivory, painter, embroiderer, and engraver, and besides these the carriers and suppliers of the materials, such as merchants, sailors, and pilots for the sea-borne traffic, and wagon-makers, trainers of draft-animals, and drivers for everything that came by land. There were also rope-makers, weavers, leather-workers, road-builders, and miners. Each individual craft, like a general with an army under his separate command, had its own corps of unskilled laborers at its disposal.[66]

There were also bakers, butchers, laundresses, potters, cobblers, doctors, and many other tradespeople. Thus, a great many Greeks, including a fair number of women, had nonagrarian occupations in Classical times, and the majority of these workers were usually much in demand. So, most such jobs became socially acceptable. (One of the few exceptions was prostitution, one of the most common female professions). Xenophon's remarks and similar sentiments voiced by Aristotle and others, therefore, reflect an outdated, rather snooty attitude perpetuated by some members of the tiny aristocratic class.

The "Noble," Hardworking Farmer

It is not surprising that Xenophon and writers like him extolled the supposedly superior virtues of farmers and tilling the soil. Xenophon was a well-to-do, conservative estate owner who felt that the old ways were

the best. Still, even in his day, when most people were more "modern" thinking, farming remained the principal basis of Greece's economy and the most widely respected profession. In this regard, most Greeks, regardless of the era they lived in, surely agreed with the opinion expressed in the following praise of farming composed by Xenophon:

> The land bears not only the means for people to live, but also . . . provides all

A vase from ancient Athens shows a shoemaker cutting leather for a shoe.

the things people use to decorate their altars. . . . The land provides the greatest abundance of good things, but doesn't allow them to be taken without effort. It trains people to endure the cold of winter and the heat of summer. It exercises and strengthens

A farmer plows his fields while helpers tend the oxen and scatter seeds.

small landowners who work it with their hands. . . . The land also plays a part in encouraging farmers to take up arms to assist their country, because its crops grow out in the open for the victor to take. . . . Agriculture also contributes to training people in cooperation. . . . Whoever it was who said that agriculture is the mother and nurse of all other arts was right, because when agriculture is faring well, all the other arts are strengthened, too. [67]

Few written descriptions (from before the Roman period) have survived of the daily routines of this predominantly male occupation that people such as Xenophon viewed as so noble. One exception is the *Works and Days* by Hesiod, a Greek farmer and poet of the early seventh century B.C. From studies of this work and other evidence, it appears that those Greek farmers who cultivated grains such as barley and wheat sowed these crops in October. This was designed to take advantage of the area's Mediterranean climate, with its long, hot summers and short, mild, but rainy winters. Planting in the fall ensured that the rainy season would give the grain plenty of moisture.

The planting was accomplished by crude wooden plows drawn by oxen or mules. Usually, the farmer guided the plow while a helper followed along tossing the seeds, which he or she carried in a sack. Sometimes another helper, often a slave, covered the seeds with dirt. Hesiod gives this advice:

Greek Blacksmiths

In this excerpt from his book about ancient Greek life, scholar Robert Flaceliere describes Greek black-smiths and their tools, based on surviving vase paintings.

The furnace is always shown as being higher than a man, at least six feet from ground to summit. The fire . . . is worked up with a bag-like bellows made from goatskin. One worker holds a piece of metal down on the anvil with a long pair of pincers, while another hammers it out. In almost all the forges thus depicted, we see one or two jars hanging from the wall. These doubtless contained water to refresh the thirsty smiths, who most often appear stark naked, or at the most very lightly clad.

When you start to plow . . . hold the [plow's] handles in your hand, and strike the oxen [with a whip or rope] as they tug the straps. A slave should follow after with a stick to hide the seeds [from] the birds. . . . If you proceed as I have described, your [grain] will nod and bow with fatness. . . . Then you'll sweep the cobwebs from your storage jars and you'll be glad. [68]

A farmer harvested his grain in April or May and threshed it (separated it from the stalks and the husks) by having mules trample it on a stone floor.

For crops such as grapes and olives, the planting and harvesting calendars were different. Farmers picked their grapes in September and then crushed them by foot (a method still in use) to make wine. In contrast, olives were harvested between October and January, either by handpicking or by using sticks to knock them out of the trees.

Many farmers supplemented both their diets and incomes by raising livestock. Sheep, goats, and pigs were the most common varieties. (Goats provided milk, cheese, and meat, and sheep the same, plus wool to make clothes.) But some farms raised chickens, donkeys, mules, cows, and oxen as well, and a few wealthier estates bred horses (used mainly for racing and warfare).

Wholesale and Retail Merchants

The farmers who raised these crops and animals continued to dominate the Greek countryside throughout ancient times. In contrast, beginning in the Classical Age, when trade and industry expanded, merchants became permanent and important fixtures of the urban centers. These workers, almost always men, were broadly divided into two groups—retail tradesmen, called *kapeloi,* and wholesale traders, known as *emporoi.* Usually, the traders were fairly well-to-do individuals who owned or leased the cargo ships that brought in goods from foreign city-states and lands. These wholesalers supplied many of the retailers, who, in their shops or stalls in the marketplace, sold them to the public.

The trader's profession was vital to the economic lifeblood of the major city-states. Athens benefited the most in Classical times because it had the largest cargo fleets (as well as the biggest navy of warships), which imported both basic and luxury goods from all over. According to the Old Oligarch, "Whatever the delicacy in Sicily, Italy, Cyprus, Egypt, Lydia, Pontus, the Peloponnesus, or anywhere else, all these have been brought together in one place by virtue of naval power."[69] Vigorous trade not only made Athens a cosmopolitan city and raised its living standards but also lined the pockets of the traders.

But though traders often made a lot of money, they earned it because their jobs were difficult and often dangerous. In some areas, pirates were a threat; and the risk of one's vessel capsizing and sinking was ever present. To avoid storms, most merchant ships avoided traveling in winter and confined their voyages to spring and summer; and when possible, they hugged the coastlines and kept land in sight. Lacking compasses, powerful lighthouses, and reliable charts, in the open sea they navigated by the sun and stars. Traders' lives were also lonely since they were away from family and friends for weeks, months, or longer. Some kept in contact via letters (which a person asked a fellow traveler who happened to be heading in the right direction to carry).

Meanwhile, the retailers in the local marketplaces sold imported products supplied by the traders and/or items grown or made locally. Food sellers, many of them farmers from the surrounding countryside, were prominent, as were fabric and clothes merchants, cobblers, booksellers, slave dealers, and artisans such as woodworkers, potters, and metalsmiths. Alfred Zimmern offers this reconstructed snapshot of Athens's crowded, noisy Agora:

> The general plan of the marketplace is a rough square. Along two sides of it there are colonnades . . . with brightly colored paintings on their inner walls. . . . About half the area of the square is kept free and open for the general public, who are already beginning to come together for the morning's chatter. The other half [of the Agora] is filled with a . . . confusion of stalls and booths . . . and sunshades, and every variety of temporary erection, roughly arranged . . . in such a chaos of men and wares and such a babel of voices . . . according to the nature of the goods being sold. The greater part of these consist of foodstuffs. . . . A new cargo from Arabia, via Egypt, reached port only yesterday, and here are subtle and exotic

scents such as the city never knew before. But the prices asked are too high. . . . Avoiding the slave market, being in no mood for an exhibition of naked humanity, we move on to the humble book stalls, hidden away by themselves in the quietest corner of the market.[70]

Books, slaves, and foreign perfumes were finished products, so to speak, that one simply bought and used as is. On the other hand, some of the merchants in the marketplace sold raw materials that craftsmen then transformed into useful everyday products. A good example is the interdependence of tanners and cobblers. The tanner (or currier) acquired animal hides and carefully scraped off the fur, hair, and fat. He then soaked the hide in a solution containing such products as tree bark, salt, and oil. Finally, he "finished" the leather by beating and coloring it. A customer bought the finished leather and took it to a cobbler, who placed it on a wooden block. The customer then placed his or her foot on the leather and the cobbler cut around it, creating a made-to-fit shoe sole, onto which the sides and top of the shoe were later stitched.

Potters and Stonemasons

Of the artisans who sold their wares in the marketplace, potters were among the most numerous and popular. In large degree this is because their wares were used by Greeks

A modern reconstruction shows how the Athenian Agora probably looked during the second half of the Classical Age. The Acropolis rises in the distance.

of all walks of life in both private and public settings. Items made of ceramics (from the Greek word *ceramos,* meaning "potter's clay") included vases for holding flowers and fruit, pitchers to pour water and wine, bowls to mix water and wine, tableware, drinking cups, sacred vessels for sacrifices, storage jars for olive oil and grain, and containers for dead people's ashes, to name only a few.

A Greek potter is hard at work in his shop in the marketplace.

The average Greek potter in the Classical Age modeled the wet clay into the desired shapes on a wheel turned by hand or by a foot peddle. He then fired it in a kiln that reached a temperature of about one thousand degrees Fahrenheit. Although these craftsmen made their products for practical use, they strove for originality of design and excellence of execution in every piece. Because most of the shapes of the pieces were fairly standard, much of the originality, as well as their attractiveness, derived from the way they were painted. A number of potters were gifted artists who captured scenes from everyday life in stunning detail and exquisite beauty, as surviving examples of their works attest.

The styles the potters employed varied from age to age. In the century preceding the Classical period, most ceramic vessels were executed in the so-called black-figure style pioneered by Athenian artisans. One was Sophilos, the first potter known to have signed his work. In black-figure items, figures of men, animals, and so forth, were painted in black on the natural buff-colored background of a fired pot. The artist then used a pointed tool to etch details into the figures. Black-figure pottery reached its height of popularity between 550 and 525 B.C. in the work of an unnamed artisan whom scholars refer to as the Amasis Painter. In the years that followed, the red-figure style was introduced and quickly gained in popularity. This technique left the figures of humans and animals in the fired pot's natural reddish tone and rendered the backgrounds black. This allowed for the application of more realistic details, which were applied with a brush (although etching was still employed for certain fine details). Red-figure pottery was perfected during the early 400s B.C. by such Athenian artisans as the so-called Berlin Painter, who excelled at portraying human limbs and muscles.

Another common skilled male profession that produced products that were both useful and attractive was stonemasonry. Stonemasons, who were always in high demand, were mostly small contractors. That is, they usually worked for themselves, turning out tombstones and cutting stones for small privately funded projects. Evidence shows that they signed contracts that ensured they would complete the work in a reasonable span of time and take responsibility for any poor workmanship. (The mason could be fired or sued for bad work.)

Sometimes, however, the state hired stonemasons to work on temples and other large-scale public buildings. Such a project might keep dozens or hundreds of masons busy for months or even several years. The basic stonework on the Acropolis's Parthenon temple alone took nine years to complete. During those years, hundreds of stonecutters labored at the marble quarries at Mt. Pentelicon in central Attica. They separated the marble from the mountainside by cutting grooves using wooden mallets and iron chisels. Into the grooves, they drove wooden wedges, which they saturated with water. As the wedges absorbed the water, they expanded, forcing the stone to

This beautifully made black-figure vase dates from about 530 B.C.

crack. Then the workers used crowbars and other tools to finish freeing the stones and turned them over to waiting crews of laborers, who moved the blocks down the mountainside and transported them to Athens.

There, on the summit of the Acropolis, the masons and their crews prepared the rough and unfinished marble blocks for use in the temple's walls. They used mallets and flat chisels to cut each stone to fit into a spot already determined and measured by one

A Stonemason's Contract

These are excerpts from a surviving contract (translated in Alfred Zimmern's The Greek Commonwealth *) negotiated between an Athenian stonemason and the government, which had hired him to work on a public temple.*

He shall work continuously . . . with a sufficient number of craftsmen [to do the job] . . . not less than five, and if he disobeys any provision written down in the agreement or be discovered executing bad work, he shall be punished by the overseers [of the building project]. . . . And if the contractor injures any sound stone in the course of his work, he shall replace it at his own expense without interruption to the work, and shall remove the spoiled stone out of the temple enclosure within five days . . . and if the contractors have any dispute among themselves upon anything written in the agreement, the overseers shall [arbitrate the dispute].

A group of stonemasons ply their trade in this second-century carving. Their skills were essential for public building projects.

of the project's foremen. This work required extreme skill and precision because no mortar was used and the stones, no two of which were exactly alike, had to fit together snugly. (After being lowered into place, they were joined to one another with I-shaped iron clamps.) Meanwhile, another group of masons prepared the stones for the temple's columns. These rounded pieces, called drums, were stacked about eleven high and were topped by a decorated piece called a capital. To cut a drum to the desired diameter, a mason placed one of the still irregular stone disks on top of a circular stone pattern already prepared on the ground. Using a mallet and a pointed metal tool, he carefully chipped away pieces of the disk until its diameter matched that of the pattern below it. After the work of the masons was complete, sculptors, metal workers, and painters added the decorative finishing touches to the building.

Respectable Women's Occupations

Most Greek women did not have occupations in the formal sense of the word, unless one defines "housekeeper" as an occupation; however, the jobs performed by women in the home—cooking, cleaning, making clothes, raising children, and so on—were seen more as traditional female duties than as occupational skills. Still, some Greek women did work outside the home. The majority of these workers were either poor citizen women or noncitizens. The noncitizens included female metics, slaves, and freedwomen. There was no particular stigma attached to these women working, as there was for middle- and upper-class citizen women. The general view was that lower-class women had to work to survive.

Various ancient sources reveal some of the occupations of Athenian female workers. A court speech written by Demosthenes, for example, mentions women who picked grapes. And the playwright Aristophanes describes women, presumably citizens, working as barmaids and selling bread, garlic, and other groceries in the marketplace. Evidence suggests that it was acceptable for women to sell these and other items in public as long as their value was small. (Expensive items were always sold by men.) It is certain that citizen women in Athens also worked as midwives, wet nurses, laundresses, and wool workers.

Noncitizen women held some or all of these same jobs. And it appears that they worked right alongside poor citizen women. This is not surprising considering that all of these groups had similar financial status and lifestyles. (Whether citizen women received more pay than noncitizens for the same jobs is unknown, but it is not likely that they did.) Surviving inscriptions made when some Athenian slave women were freed mention their occupations. These included a sesame-seed seller, wet nurse, grocer, perfume vendor, cloak seller, salt vendor, shoe seller, honey seller, horse tender, flute player, and several wool workers.

Tombstone epitaphs discovered in Athens and other parts of the Greek world list some of these same female occupations, wool workers and midwives being particularly common.

Playing the flute was a common female profession.

One epitaph from the fourth century B.C. mentions a profession that was surely far less common for women—doctor: "Phanostrate, a midwife and physician, lies here. She caused pain to none, and all lamented her death."[71]

It is unclear how she managed to enter a trade dominated by men. Nor is it known whom she treated and how the community accepted her. Also exceptional was a female pottery painter depicted in a scene on a fifth-century B.C. Athenian vase. She was probably the wife, daughter, or slave of a metic since most of the artisans in Athens were metics. There is an outside chance, of course, that noncitizen female artisans' assistants may not have been all that uncommon, but they were not often depicted in art or mentioned in inscriptions.

Less Respectable Women's Occupations

Poor, noncitizen, and slave women who worked as midwives, laundresses, food sellers, and so on labored in what society viewed as morally acceptable occupations. In contrast, some women worked in jobs that were widely seen as disreputable—prostitute (including the high-class variety, the courtesan) and entertainer. These professions were not only legal but in high demand in nearly all Greek cities. This reflects a clear double standard of the male-dominated Greek order, in which society held prostitutes and entertainers in contempt, yet men paid for their services on a regular basis. In one of his speeches, Demosthenes sums up this seemingly contradictory social reality: "Courtesans we keep for pleasure . . . but wives for the procreation of legitimate children and to be our faithful housekeepers."[72] The Athenian government accepted rather than fought this reality; it set the maximum prices prostitutes could charge and taxed their income.

Ancient Greek prostitutes, like those in other places and times, could be both low class and cheap and high class and expensive. Common prostitutes (*pornai*) usually frequented the "red-light" districts, areas in which they and other social outcasts congregated. In Athens these were the Ceramicus, the area in which many of the potters' shops were located; and parts of the port town of Piraeus. These prostitutes worked in brothels or stood in the streets waiting for men to hire them. Those in the brothels were likely slaves owned by the men who ran these businesses, whereas the streetwalkers were freedwomen, metics, or on occasion poor citizen women. Few descriptions of common Greek prostitutes have survived. This one, from a fragment of a work by the fourth-century B.C. comic playwright Xenarchus, describes the seamy atmosphere of a brothel:

[Customers] are not banned from looking at [the girls] as they sun-bathe with bare breasts, stripped for action in semicircular ranks; and from among these ladies you can select whichever one you like: thin, fat, round, tall, short, young, old, middle-aged or past it. . . . With these girls you're the one that gets grabbed. They positively pull you inside, calling the old men "Little Daddies" and the younger ones "Little Brothers." And any one of them is available, without risk, without expense, in the daytime, in the evening, any way you want it. [73]

Meanwhile, at the upper level of the sexual market were the high-class courtesans, the *hetairai*, or "companions." In Athens they were usually foreigners who received good pay for entertaining men either in rented houses or rooms (paid for by either the men or the courtesans themselves) or in the men's homes. These women commanded higher status and fees than ordinary prostitutes because they provided men with more than just sex. First, such women were educated, often better than the men they worked for. So they could discuss politics, philosophy, art, science, and other subjects about which the men's wives knew very little. To most Greek men, a woman who could stimulate them both physically and intellectually was very enticing. (Yet sadly, tradition and custom forbade wives from fulfilling this role.)

High class prostitutes often attended symposia like the one depicted on this ancient vase.

Because Greek men frowned on female independence and excluded women from formal education, courtesans were the most economically independent women in society. One of the most intelligent, educated, and successful courtesans in the Classical Age was Aspasia from the city of Miletus (in Asia Minor). After Pericles, the leading Athenian statesman of the fifth century B.C., divorced his wife, he asked Aspasia to move into his house, and they remained together until his death in 429 B.C. Pericles' political enemies often denounced them both, calling the situation immoral. But it appears the relationship was driven by deep love and mutual commitment, much as in the modern ideal, which made it extremely unusual for its time and place. They not only had a child together (who was, of course, illegitimate), but it seems that Pericles was not averse to listening to Aspasia's political advice. He was attracted to her "because of her rare political wisdom," Plutarch wrote. She was so well informed and witty that the philosopher Socrates

visited her from time to time with his disciples, and some of his close friends brought their wives to listen to her conversation. . . . Pericles' attachment to Aspasia seems to have been a more passionate affair. . . . He loved [her] dearly. The story goes that every day, when he went out to the marketplace and returned, he greeted her with a kiss. [74]

Once more, restrictive traditions kept some Greeks from fulfilling their personal potentials while strengthening and enriching society as a whole. Aspasia became a high-class prostitute because it was the only position in which society allowed her intellectual talents and vibrant personality to shine. Today, women of her caliber become college professors, best-selling writers, judges, senators, and heads of state. Had Aspasia and other talented Greek women enjoyed equal professional opportunities with men, Greece would have been transformed, and with it, perhaps, the world.

Notes

Introduction: The Mute Stones Speak: Evidence for Greek Life

1. Thomas R. Martin, *Ancient Greece: From Prehistoric to Hellenistic Times.* New Haven, CT: Yale University Press, 1996, p. 124.
2. Quoted in Thucydides, *The Peloponnesian War,* trans. Rex Warner. New York: Penguin, 1972, pp. 147–48.
3. Quoted in Mary R. Lefkowitz and Maureen B. Fant, eds., *Women's Life in Greece and Rome: A Source Book in Translation.* Baltimore: Johns Hopkins University Press, 1992, p. 206.

Chapter 1: Houses: Their Structure, Layout, and Contents

4. Demosthenes, *On Organization,* in *Olynthiacs, Philippics, Minor Speeches,* trans. J.H. Vince. Cambridge, MA: Harvard University Press, 1985, p. 375.
5. R.E. Wycherley, *How the Greeks Built Cities.* New York: W.W. Norton, 1962, pp. 175–77.
6. Quoted in Plutarch, *Life of Demosthenes,* in *The Age of Alexander: Nine Greek Lives by Plutarch,* trans. Ian Scott-Kilvert. New York: Penguin, 1973, pp. 197–98.
7. Xenophon, *Memorabilia,* in *Xenophon: Conversations of Socrates,*

trans. Hugh Tredennick and Robin Waterfield. New York: Penguin, 1990, p. 160.
8. Wycherley, *How the Greeks Built Cities,* pp. 180, 188–89.
9. Plato, *Symposium,* trans. W. Hamilton. Baltimore: Penguin, 1951, pp. 38–39.
10. Xenophon, *Symposium,* in *Xenophon,* p. 230.
11. Pausanias, *Guide to Greece,* vol. 1, trans. Peter Levi. New York: Penguin, 1971, p. 111.
12. Wycherley, *How the Greeks Built Cities,* p. 199.

Chapter 2: The Family: Men's vs. Women's Roles

13. Xenophon, *Oeconomicus,* in *Xenophon,* p. 311.
14. Xenophon, *Oeconomicus,* in *Xenophon,* pp. 314–15.
15. Cornelius Nepos, *The Book of the Great Generals of Foreign Nations,* trans. John Rolfe. Cambridge, MA: Harvard University Press, 1960, p. 371.
16. Xenophon, *Oeconomicus,* in *Xenophon,* p. 311.
17. Sue Blundell, *Women in Ancient Greece.* Cambridge, MA: Harvard University Press, 1995, pp. 115–16.
18. Robert Flaceliere, *Daily Life in Greece at the Time of Pericles,* trans.

Peter Green. London: Phoenix, 1996, pp. 62–64.

19. Blundell, *Women in Ancient Greece,* p. 151.

20. Plutarch, *Life of Agis,* in *Plutarch on Sparta,* trans. Richard J.A. Talbert. New York: Penguin, 1988, p. 58.

21. Plutarch, *Life of Lycurgus,* in *Plutarch on Sparta,* pp. 25–26.

Chapter 3: The Family: Children and Education

22. Mark Golden, *Children and Childhood in Classical Athens.* Baltimore: Johns Hopkins University Press, 1990, p. 94.

23. Blundell, *Women in Ancient Greece,* p. 111.

24. Golden, *Children and Childhood in Classical Athens,* p. 89.

25. Alfred Zimmern, *The Greek Commonwealth: Politics and Economics in Fifth-Century Athens,* rev. ed. 1931; reprint, New York: Oxford University Press, 1961, p. 74.

26. Plato, *Laws,* in *Plato,* trans. Benjamin Jowett. Chicago: Encyclopaedia Britannica, 1952, p. 723.

27. Aristophanes, *Clouds,* in *The Complete Plays of Aristophanes,* trans. Moses Hadas. New York: Bantam, 1962, p. 125.

28. Golden, *Children and Childhood in Classical Athens,* p. 35.

29. Plato, *Protagoras,* in *Plato,* p. 46.

30. Flaceliere, *Daily Life in Greece at the Time of Pericles,* p. 97.

31. Flaceliere, *Daily Life in Greece at the Time of Pericles,* p. 94.

32. Plutarch, *Lycurgus,* in *Plutarch on Sparta,* pp. 28–29.

33. Plutarch, *Lycurgus,* in *Plutarch on Sparta,* p. 29.

34. Quoted in Lefkowitz and Fant, *Women's Life in Greece and Rome,* p. 31.

35. Plutarch, *Lycurgus,* in *Plutarch on Sparta,* p. 24.

Chapter 4: Slaves: Their Roles in the Home and in Society

36. Aristotle, *Politics,* trans. J.A. Sinclair. Baltimore: Penguin, 1962, p. 94.

37. Xenophon, *Oeconomicus,* in *Xenophon,* p. 334.

38. Quoted in Thomas Wiedemann, ed., *Greek and Roman Slavery.* Baltimore: Johns Hopkins University Press, 1981, p. 228.

39. Aristotle, *Politics,* p. 19.

40. Xenophon, *Oeconomicus,* in *Xenophon,* p. 323.

41. Xenophon, *Oeconomicus,* in *Xenophon,* p. 326.

42. Quoted in Wiedemann, *Greek and Roman Slavery,* p. 225.

43. Aristotle, *Politics,* p. 74.

44. Aristotle, *Athenian Constitution,* trans. H. Rackham. 1952; reprint, Cambridge, MA: Harvard University Press, 1996, p. 139.

45. Quoted in Wiedemann, *Greek and Roman Slavery,* p. 157.

46. Plutarch, *Lycurgus,* in *Plutarch on Sparta,* pp. 40–41.

47. Plutarch, *Lycurgus,* in *Plutarch on Sparta,* p. 41.

48. Quoted in Kathleen Freeman, *The Murder of Herodes and Other Trials from the Athenian Law Courts*. New York: W.W. Norton, 1963, p. 110.

49. Quoted in Freeman, *Murder of Herodes*, p. 74.

50. Pseudo-Xenophon (or the "Old Oligarch"), *Constitution of the Athenians*, in Xenophon, *Scripta Minora*, trans. E.C. Marchant. Cambridge, MA: Harvard University Press, 1993, p. 481.

51. Quoted in Wiedemann, *Greek and Roman Slavery*, p. 47.

52. Quoted in Wiedemann, *Greek and Roman Slavery*, p. 47.

Chapter 5: Home Life: Food, Clothes, and Private Worship

53. Andrew Dalby, *Siren Feasts: A History of Food and Gastronomy in Greece*. New York: Routledge, 1996, p. 3.

54. Homer, *Odyssey*, trans. E.V. Rieu. Baltimore: Penguin, 1961, p. 62.

55. Quoted in Plato, *Phaedrus*, in *Plato*, p. 683.

56. Euripides, *Iphigenia in Taurus*, in *Three Plays*, trans. Philip Vellacott. Baltimore: Penguin, 1968, p. 112.

57. Plato, *Republic*, in *Plato*, pp. 313–14.

58. Dalby, *Siren Feasts*, p. 28.

59. Dalby, *Siren Feasts*, p. 23.

60. Lesley Adkins and Roy A. Adkins, *Handbook to Life in Ancient Greece*. New York: Facts On File, 1997, p. 175.

61. Flaceliere, *Daily Life in Greece at the Time of Pericles*, p. 154.

62. Plato, *Theaetetus*, in *Plato*, p. 530.

63. Sarah B. Pomeroy, *Goddesses, Whores, Wives, and Slaves: Women in Classical Antiquity*. New York: Shocken, 1975, p. 83.

64. Xenophon, *Oeconomicus*, in *Xenophon*, p. 325.

Chapter 6: Work: Common Male and Female Occupations

65. Xenophon, *Oeconomicus*, in *Xenophon*, pp. 300–301.

66. Plutarch, *Life of Pericles*, in *The Rise and Fall of Athens: Nine Greek Lives by Plutarch*, trans. Ian Scott-Kilvert. New York: Penguin, 1960, pp. 78–79.

67. Xenophon, *Oeconomicus*, in *Xenophon*, pp. 305–307.

68. Hesiod, *Works and Days*, in *Hesiod and Theognis*, trans. Dorothea Wender. New York: Penguin, 1973, pp. 73–74.

69. Quoted in Xenophon, *Scripta Minora*, p. 491.

70. Zimmern, *The Greek Commonwealth*, pp. 281–82.

71. Quoted in Lefkowitz and Fant, *Women's Life in Greece and Rome*, p. 267.

72. Quoted in Freeman, *Murder of Herodes*, p. 221.

73. Quoted in James Davidson, *Courtesans and Fishcakes: The Consuming Passions of Classical Athens*. New York: St. Martin's, 1998, p. 84.

74. Plutarch, *Pericles*, in *The Rise and Fall of Athens*, pp. 190–91.

Glossary

acropolis: "The city's high place"; a hill, usually fortified, central to many Greek towns; the term in upper case (Acropolis) refers to the one in Athens.

agoge: The regimented system of education and military training in Sparta.

agora: A Greek marketplace; the term in upper case (Agora) refers to the one in Athens.

akratisma: Breakfast.

amphidromia: A postbirth ceremony in which relatives and friends sent gifts to the newborn's family.

andron: A room in which the master of a house dined and entertained guests.

archon: A public administrator in Athens.

ariston: A light lunch.

astai (singular, *aste*): Citizens who lacked political rights (most often applied to women).

brazier: A metal container that burned wood or charcoal, used for cooking and heating.

capital: The decorative top piece of a column.

ceramos: Potter's clay.

chiton: A basic tunic.

chlamys: An outer cloak or cape worn by young men and soldiers.

colonnade: A row of columns.

crater (*krater*): A container for mixing wine and water.

decate: A postbirth ceremony in which parents named the newborn.

deipnon: Supper.

divination: The reading and interpretation of omens and other divine signs.

drum: A single cylindrical component of a column.

emporoi: Wholesale traders.

engue: A formal betrothal, usually conducted in front of witnesses.

epikleros: "Without property"; a Greek heiress who had to marry an uncle or cousin in order to receive her father's legacy.

exedra: A sitting room in a Greek house, usually adjoining the courtyard.

exposure: The practice of leaving a newborn infant outside to die.

fountain house: A small building, built beside a stream or fed by an aqueduct, that dispensed water to people who lived nearby.

freedman: A slave who gained his or her freedom.

gamos: A wedding celebration.

grammatistes: Teachers of reading, writing, and simple mathematics.

gynaeceum: The women's quarters of a Greek home.

helots: Spartan slaves.

herm: A bust of the god Hermes placed near the front door of a house to ward off evil.

hetairai: "Companions"; high-class prostitutes; educated women who provided men with sex and intelligent conversation.

himation: A large outer cloak.

kapeloi: Retail merchants and craftsmen.

kitharistes: Music teachers.

kyrios: A woman's male guardian, usually her father or husband.

libation: A liquid sacrifice.

lyre (*lyra*): A small harp.

maia: A midwife.

metics (*metoikoi*): Foreigners (either Greeks from other city-states or non-Greeks) living in Athens.

moicheia: Adultery.

oikos (plural, *oikoi*): The family.

omen: A sign of impending good or bad fortune.

paidagogos: A slave or freedman who accompanied a boy to school and supervised his behavior there.

paidotribes: Athletic instructors or coaches.

pastas: A long central hallway in a Greek house.

perioikoi: "Dwellers round about"; resident foreigners in Sparta.

petasos: A hat with a broad brim.

phiale: A bowl for sacrificial liquids.

phratry: "Blood brotherhood"; an extended kinship group composed of about thirty clans.

politai: Citizens with political rights.

polluted: Religiously unclean or tainted.

pornai: Common prostitutes.

symposium (plural, symposia): An after-dinner party, usually in a private home.

terra-cotta: Baked clay.

thysia: Sacrifice, especially of animals.

For Further Reading

Books

Robert E. Hull, *The World of Ancient Greece: Religion and the Gods.* New York: Franklin Watts, 2000. A handsomely illustrated look at ancient Greek religion.

Robert B. Kebric, *Greek People.* Mountain View, CA: Mayfield, 2001. A superb overview of major ancient Greek figures from all walks of life.

Vicki Leon, *Uppity Women of Ancient Times.* Berkeley, CA: Conari, 1995. A highly entertaining book that tells the stories of famous women and their struggles during ancient times.

Don Nardo, *Greek Temples.* New York: Franklin Watts, 2002. A colorfully illustrated overview of how Greek temples were built and used. Written for younger readers.

——, *Greenhaven Encyclopedia of Greek and Roman Mythology.* San Diego: Greenhaven, 2002. Contains hundreds of short but informative articles on Greek myths, gods, heroes, and the myth tellers and their works.

——, *Women of Ancient Greece.* San Diego: Lucent Books, 2000. A detailed look at all aspects of the lives of women in the ancient Greek city-states.

Internet Sources

Kristina Bagwell, "Burial Rituals and the Afterlife of Ancient Greece," University of North Carolina. http://people.uncw. edu/deagona/ancientnovel/Kristina. htm. An attractive, worthwhile general overview of two aspects of ancient Greek life related to religion.

Hellenic Museum and Cultural Center, "A Day in the Life of an Ancient Greek." www.hellenicmuseum.org/exhibits/day inlife.html. A useful, easy-to-read general source for ancient Greek life, including clothes, food, sports, art, and more.

Tufts University Department of the Classics, "Perseus Project." www.perseus.tufts.edu. The most comprehensive online source about ancient Greece, with hundreds of links to all aspects of Greek history, life, and culture, supported by numerous photos of artifacts.

Works Consulted

Major Works

Sue Blundell, *Women in Ancient Greece.* Cambridge, MA: Harvard University Press, 1995. One of the best general works on ancient Greek women presently available.

Walter Burkert, *Greek Religion, Archaic and Classical.* Oxford, UK: Basil Blackwell, 1985. The classic secondary work on Greek religion.

Andrew Dalby, *Siren Feasts: A History of Food and Gastronomy in Greece.* New York: Routledge, 1996. An informative and highly entertaining overview of ancient Greek foods, cooking, and eating habits.

N.R.E. Fisher, *Social Values in Classical Athens.* London: Dent, 1976. Contains a brief but informative overview of Athenian social customs, along with several supporting primary source documents.

——, *Slavery in Classical Greece.* London: Bristol Classical, 1993. An excellent synopsis of Greek slaves, their lives, and their struggles.

Robert Flaceliere, *Daily Life in Greece at the Time of Pericles.* Trans. Peter Green. London: Phoenix, 1996. One of the best available general overviews of ancient Greek life and social customs.

Mark Golden, *Children and Childhood in Classical Athens.* Baltimore: Johns Hopkins University Press, 1990. This detailed, well-documented study of the lives of ancient Athenian girls and boys will appeal mainly to scholars and serious students of ancient Greece.

Michael Grant, *A Social History of Greece and Rome.* New York: Scribner's, 1992. A clearly written general study of ancient Greek and Roman women, freedwomen, slaves, rich people, poor people, and so on.

John D. Mikalson, *Athenian Popular Religion.* Chapel Hill: University of North Carolina Press, 1983. A detailed study of religious beliefs and worship in ancient Athens.

Sarah B. Pomeroy, *Families in Classical and Hellenistic Greece.* New York: Oxford University Press, 1999. A superior overview of the ancient Greek family by one of the world's leading classical scholars.

R.E. Wycherley, *How the Greeks Built Cities.* New York: W.W. Norton, 1962. The classic work on ancient Greek city planning, houses, fortifications, and fountain houses.

Alfred Zimmern, *The Greek Commonwealth: Politics and Economics in Fifth-Century Athens.* Rev. ed. 1931. Reprint, New York: Oxford University Press, 1961. A detailed, thoughtful, and acclaimed reconstruction of the way the Greeks lived and thought in the Classical Age.

Other Important Works

Primary Sources

Aeschylus, Oresteia trilogy, in *Aeschylus I: Oresteia*. Trans. Richmond Lattimore. Chicago: University of Chicago Press, 1953.

Aristophanes, *The Complete Plays of Aristophanes*. Trans. Moses Hadas. New York: Bantam, 1962.

Aristotle, *Athenian Constitution*. Trans. H. Rackham. 1952. Reprint, Cambridge, MA: Harvard University Press, 1996

———, *Politics*. Trans. J.A. Sinclair. Baltimore: Penguin, 1962.

Demosthenes, *Olynthiacs, Philippics, Minor Speeches*. Trans. J.H. Vince. Cambridge, MA: Harvard University Press, 1985.

Euripides, *Three Plays*. Trans. Philip Vellacott. Baltimore: Penguin, 1968.

Kathleen Freeman, *The Murder of Herodes and Other Trials from the Athenian Law Courts*. New York: W.W. Norton, 1963.

Hesiod, *Theogony* and *Works and Days,* in *Hesiod and Theognis*. Trans. Dorothea Wender. New York: Penguin, 1973.

Homer, *Iliad*. Trans. E.V. Rieu. Baltimore: Penguin, 1950.

———, *Odyssey*. Trans. E.V. Rieu. Baltimore: Penguin, 1961.

Mary R. Lefkowitz and Maureen B. Fant, eds., *Women's Life in Greece and Rome: A Source Book in Translation*.

Baltimore: Johns Hopkins University Press, 1992.

Cornelius Nepos, *The Book of the Great Generals of Foreign Nations*. Trans. John Rolfe. Cambridge, MA: Harvard University Press, 1960.

Pausanias, *Guide to Greece*. 2 vols. Trans. Peter Levi. New York: Penguin, 1971.

Pindar, *Odes*. Trans. C.M. Bowra. New York: Penguin, 1969.

Plato, dialogues and other works in *Plato*. Trans. Benjamin Jowett. Chicago: Encyclopaedia Britannica, 1952; and *Symposium*. Trans. W. Hamilton. Baltimore: Penguin, 1951.

Plutarch, *Parallel Lives,* excerpted in *The Rise and Fall of Athens: Nine Greek Lives by Plutarch*. Trans. Ian Scott-Kilvert. New York: Penguin, 1960; and excerpted in *The Age of Alexander: Nine Greek Lives by Plutarch*. Trans. Ian Scott-Kilvert. New York: Penguin, 1973.

———, assorted works in *Plutarch on Sparta*. Trans. Richard J.A. Talbert. New York: Penguin, 1988.

Thucydides, *The Peloponnesian War*. Trans. Rex Warner. New York: Penguin, 1972.

Thomas Wiedemann, ed., *Greek and Roman Slavery*. Baltimore: Johns Hopkins University Press, 1981.

Xenophon, *Memorabilia, Oeconomicus,* and *Symposium,* in *Xenophon: Conversations of Socrates*. Trans. Hugh Tredennick and Robin Waterfield. New York: Penguin, 1990.

———, *Scripta Minora*. Trans. E.C. Marchant. Cambridge, MA: Harvard University Press, 1993.

Modern Sources

Lesley Adkins and Roy A. Adkins, *Handbook to Life in Ancient Greece.* New York: Facts On File, 1997.

Alison Burford, *Land and Labor in the Greek World.* Baltimore: Johns Hopkins University Press, 1993.

Eva Cantarella, *Pandora's Daughters: The Role and Status of Women in Greek and Roman Antiquity.* Trans. Maureen B. Fant. Baltimore: Johns Hopkins University Press, 1987.

James Davidson, *Courtesans and Fishcakes: The Consuming Passions of Classical Athens.* New York: St. Martin's, 1998.

Charles Freeman, *The Greek Achievement: The Foundation of the Western World.* New York: Viking, 1999.

Frank J. Frost, *Greek Society.* Lexington, MA: D.C. Heath, 1980.

Victor D. Hanson, *The Other Greeks: The Family Farm and the Agrarian Roots of Western Civilization.* New York: Simon and Schuster, 1995.

S.C. Humphrey, *The Family, Women, and Death.* Ann Arbor: University of Michigan Press, 1993.

Joint Association of Classical Teachers, *The World of Athens: An Introduction to Classical Athenian Culture.* New York: Cambridge University Press, 1984.

W.K. Lacey, *The Family in Classical Greece.* London: Thames and Hudson, 1968.

Thomas R. Martin, *Ancient Greece: From Prehistoric to Hellenistic Times.* New Haven, CT: Yale University Press, 1996.

Jennifer Neils, *Goddess and Polis: The Panathenaic Festival in Ancient Athens.* Princeton, NJ: Princeton University Press, 1992.

Sarah B. Pomeroy, *Goddesses, Whores, Wives, and Slaves: Women in Classical Antiquity.* New York: Shocken, 1975.

———, *Women in Hellenistic Egypt: From Alexander to Cleopatra.* New York: Shocken, 1989.

Sarah B. Pomeroy et al., *Ancient Greece: A Political, Social, and Cultural History.* New York: Oxford University Press, 1999.

C.E. Robinson, *Everyday Life in Ancient Greece.* Oxford, UK: Clarendon, 1968.

Raphael Sealey, *Women and Law in Classical Greece.* Chapel Hill: University of North Carolina Press, 1990.

Index

Picture Credits

About the Author

Historian Don Nardo has written or edited numerous volumes about the ancient Greek world, including *Greek and Roman Sport, The Age of Pericles, The Parthenon, Life in Ancient Athens, The Decline and Fall of Ancient Greece,* and literary companions to the works of Homer, Euripides, and Sophocles. He resides with his wife, Christine, in Massachusetts.